AYN RAND

AN INTRODUCTION

EAMONN BUTLER

Institute of
Economic Affairs

First published in Great Britain in 2018 by
The Institute of Economic Affairs
2 Lord North Street
Westminster
London SW1P 3LB
in association with London Publishing Partnership Ltd
www.londonpublishingpartnership.co.uk

The mission of the Institute of Economic Affairs is to improve understanding
of the fundamental institutions of a free society by analysing and expounding
the role of markets in solving economic and social problems.

A CIP catalogue record for this book is available from the British Library.

ISBN 978-0-255-36764-6

Many IEA publications are translated into languages other
than English or are reprinted. Permission to translate or to reprint
should be sought from the Director General at the address above.

Typeset in Kepler by T&T Productions Ltd
www.tandtproductions.com

Printed and bound in Great Britain by Hobbs the Printers Ltd

This book is addressed to the young – in years or in spirit – who are not afraid to know and are not ready to give up.
Ayn Rand, *Capitalism: The Unknown Ideal*

CONTENTS

THE AUTHOR

Eamonn Butler is Director of the Adam Smith Institute, one of the world's leading policy think tanks. He holds degrees in economics and psychology, a PhD in philosophy, and an honorary DLitt. In the 1970s he worked in Washington for the US House of Representatives, and taught philosophy at Hillsdale College, Michigan, before returning to the UK to help found the Adam Smith Institute. A former winner of the Freedom Medal awarded by Freedom's Foundation of Valley Forge and the UK National Free Enterprise Award, Eamonn is currently Secretary of the Mont Pelerin Society.

Eamonn is author of many books, including introductions to the pioneering economists and thinkers Adam Smith, Milton Friedman, F. A. Hayek and Ludwig von Mises. He has also published primers on classical liberalism, public choice, Magna Carta, the Austrian School of Economics and great liberal thinkers, as well as *The Condensed Wealth of Nations* and *The Best Book on the Market*. His *Foundations of a Free Society* won the 2014 Fisher Prize. He is co-author of *Forty Centuries of Wage and Price Controls*, and of a series of books on IQ. He is a frequent contributor to print, broadcast and online media.

ACKNOWLEDGEMENTS

Thanks go to Carl Barney and Yaron Brook for their encouragement on this project and to Greg Salmieri and Mike Berliner for their extremely helpful criticisms on the draft.

1 INTRODUCTION

What this book is about

This book guides the reader through the highly original, but controversial, ideas of the Russian–American writer and thinker Ayn Rand (1905–82) – best known for her 'Objectivist' worldview and her novels *The Fountainhead* (1943) and *Atlas Shrugged* (1957).

Rand's thinking still has profound influence, particularly on those who come to it through her novels, attracted by their core messages of individualism, self-worth, and the right to live your life without others imposing on you. The hunger for this vision seems limitless. *Atlas Shrugged* sells almost a quarter of a million copies annually – quite remarkable for a book of 1,200 pages, published more than half a century ago – with sales of *The Fountainhead* not far behind. Their popularity has made Rand the top recruiter for the individualist movement. In the famous words of one libertarian activist, 'It usually begins with Ayn Rand.'

This has made her a major influence on many of the world's leading legislators, policy advisers, and economists. Entrepreneurs and investors too, particularly those leading the knowledge industries (such as Wikipedia co-founder Jimmy Wales and PayPal co-founder Peter Thiel), have been inspired by her robust account of the morality of free-market capitalism, and of the crucial role of creative minds in driving human progress.

More widely, though, Rand's ideas remain highly controversial – or deeply unfashionable. Academics largely ignore her thoughts on art, literature, and philosophy. Traditionalists find her attacks on altruism and religion shocking. Progressives scorn her view of state intervention as a destroyer of value, spirit and life itself. Public intellectuals dismiss her as a crazy extremist whose work fuels the worst vices of greed, self-absorption, indifference, and callousness.

Such reactions should come as no surprise. Rand herself radically and intensely opposed almost every strand of mainstream thinking – on human nature, morality, politics, economics, art, literature, education, and even reality itself. Yet her positions were all part of a consistent and comprehensive view of life and the universe. It is a view that should be taken seriously, no matter how unorthodox and shocking it might seem.

Even if you disagree with Ayn Rand, she certainly makes you think.

What this book covers

This book is shorter than the 32,963-word speech by the character John Galt in *Atlas Shrugged*, which encapsulates Rand's worldview. So it must focus on the essentials, avoiding academic detail. It aims only to introduce and explain Rand's key ideas, and some of the criticisms made of them, clearly and jargon free.

The book covers Rand's importance, her understanding of reality and human nature, and her conclusions on knowledge, morality, politics, economics, government, public issues, aesthetics, and literature. It places these in the context of her life and times, showing how revolutionary they were, and how they influenced the public policy debate and encouraged a spreading rejection of collectivism, centralism and statism.

Who this book is for

Rand's output covered so many subjects in so many different forms – novels, articles, speeches, interviews, books, plays, movie scripts, newsletters, broadcasts – that it can be hard to know where to begin. This book organizes her thinking into a short, structured guide.

The book is written for intelligent readers who are interested in the public debate on politics, government, social institutions, capitalism, rights, liberty, and morality. It is for anyone who wants to understand the pro-freedom side of the debate and the influence that Ayn Rand had on it through her writings, as well as through her extraordinary personality and the 'radical individualist' movement that sprang up around her.

The book aims to explain Rand's ideas in plain language, without distortion. Hence there are no academic-style footnotes or references – just an essential reading list of her most significant books and articles, ordered so that the reader can navigate them more easily.

It also gives high-school and college students of economics, politics, ethics, and philosophy a concise study guide to a set of radical ideas and opinions that are frequently dismissed or ignored by mainstream teachers. There is plenty in here to challenge those teachers!

There is also much of political interest. Rand was one of the main intellectual inspirations behind the rise of individualist, pro-freedom politics at the end of the twentieth century. Even today, her ideas influence policy around the globe.

Rand, the author and this book

I never knew Ayn Rand but, like many others, came to her when young, through her novels. I found *The Fountainhead* fresh, uplifting, and inspiring and admired its heroic vision of human creativity, achievement, and integrity. *Atlas Shrugged* moved me less. Its plot seemed far-fetched, its characters cardboard, its tone sermonizing, and its length wearing.

Moreover, I was never convinced by Rand's certainty about the nature of reality and its power to reveal truths about individuals, society and morality. And like many others at the time, I was put off by the sectarianism that surrounded her, and the schisms that continued after her death.

But today such disputes are eclipsed by the accelerating global interest in Rand's ideas, and I have returned to those ideas with an open but critical mind. I remain a skeptic, and my view of her novels is unchanged. But I hope that my personal opinions do not color what follows, and that my portrayal of Rand's ideas (and some of the critical responses to them) is fair and (dare I say it?) *objective*.

How this book is structured

This book is not a chronological history but is structured around Rand's key ideas.

It begins with the question of why Rand is important and worth reading more about. It looks at her wider effect through her novels and the challenges that she posed to mainstream thinking. It then provides a brief sketch of her life and how events shaped her ideas, and how in turn those ideas shaped the lives of her followers and the world beyond. It includes a timeline of the key events and publications of her life.

Next, the book outlines the key elements of Rand's worldview. It then looks more closely at her ideas on those elements: reality, knowledge, morality, politics and public issues, economics, art and literature.

In its closing chapters, the book reviews Rand's novels, providing a guide for the reader and showing how their themes, plots, characterization, and style reflect and express her worldview. It looks at some of the criticisms that have been made of her work. It ends with a short assessment of Rand's continuing influence, a guide to further reading, and some of the key quotations that sum up her remarkably radical ideas on reality and human nature.

2 WHY AYN RAND IS IMPORTANT

The importance of Rand's fiction

It must be the most common opening of all the letters received by Rand's publishers, not to mention the many articles and blog posts about Rand that appear daily: '*Atlas
Shrugged* changed my life.'

Most people discover Rand not through her articles, but
through her fiction. Her novels have brought her ideas on
life, politics, and morality into popular culture and made
them accessible to a lay public who might struggle to wade
through some academic treatise.

Young people in particular connect easily with *The Fountainhead* and *Atlas Shrugged*, which speak to their concerns
about their future lives and ambitions. The books also feed
their natural rebelliousness, giving them the arguments
they need to challenge the received wisdom of self-sacrifice
and soft socialism that is handed down by their teachers.

Aspiring to excel

These novels feed the self-esteem of young people – and
indeed many who are not so young. They convince readers

that, through thought and action, they can create a world in which their efforts will be valued, not disparaged or exploited. They assert the nobility of using your mind to reach your full potential. They make self-belief cool.

Rand's heroes are individualists who live by their own creative talents – existing for no one else nor asking others to exist for them. They are rebels against the establishment and its ways. They do not conform to social norms but stand by their own vision and truth: a vision built on their own values and a truth built on fact and reason, not on the false authority of others. They are the creative minds who discover new knowledge, innovate, drive progress, and consequently benefit all humanity.

But minds cannot be forced to think. Creativity, and therefore human progress, depends on people being free to think and act in pursuit of their own values and on the basis of fact, not authority – a seductive idea, especially for Rand's young readers.

A comprehensive view

Another quality that makes Rand so influential is that she provides a *system* – a comprehensive view of how the world and human life work. She looks far deeper and wider than mere politics or economics, tracing their roots down to culture, society, and philosophy.

Her novels teach the ideas of liberty, values, mind, reason, creativity, entrepreneurship, capitalism, achievement, heroism, happiness, self-esteem, and pride. They explain the life-destroying consequences of coercion, extortion, regulation, self-sacrifice, altruism, wishful thinking, and refusing to use one's mind.

This is exactly what so many young people (in particular) are looking for: a comprehensive, consistent worldview that provides a way of understanding the world and a set of principles through which its many puzzles might be solved.

In time, of course, they may come across other viewpoints, or come to accept that the world is more complicated than Rand suggests. But it is a mark of the power of her system that it typically still continues to affect her readers. Their lives remain forever changed.

The spread of Rand's ideas

Nowhere do Rand's ideas change more lives than in her adopted United States, where her novels tap into the American ideals of self-reliance and individualism. In the early 1990s, a decade after her death, a survey by the Library of Congress and the Book of the Month Club rated *Atlas Shrugged* as the most influential book after the Bible. Today, Rand's ideas are taught in colleges across America and discussed in academic and popular journals. Institutes and groups have been set up to promote her ideas.

Her ideas are accelerating in other English-speaking countries too, such as the United Kingdom (where 20,000 Rand books are sold each year), Canada, Australia, New Zealand, South Africa, and India, where English is widely spoken. Even Indian footballers and Bollywood stars acknowledge her influence on their lives.

Beyond the English-speaking countries, Sweden, a country of just 9.5 million people, leads the world in Google searches for 'Ayn Rand,' and Swedes bought over 30,000 copies of her books in the last decade. About 25,000 more are bought each year in Rand's native Russia, another 13,000 a year in Brazil, 6,000 in Spain, and 1,000 each in Japan and Bulgaria. Even in China, some 15,000 Rand books are bought each year – a number which, given that country's economic and intellectual awakening, can only increase.

Influence on politics

All this gives Rand a significant impact on the political debate. In the US, many of those she inspired rose into public office. Former US Federal Reserve chairman Alan Greenspan was an early member of Rand's inner circle. Supreme Court Justice Clarence Thomas shows his new clerks the film of *The Fountainhead*. Politicians such as former Congressman Ron Paul; his son, Senator Rand Paul; and House Speaker Paul Ryan cite Rand as an influence. Even President Ronald Reagan described himself as 'an admirer of Ayn Rand.'

Nor is this only a US phenomenon. Annie Lööf, leader of Sweden's Center Party and former enterprise minister, helped launch the Swedish translation of *The Fountainhead*, calling Rand 'one of the greatest thinkers of the 20th Century.' Rand's ideas were praised by the reformist Prime Minister of Estonia, Mart Laar, and influenced Australia's

Prime Minister Malcolm Fraser, along with many other past or current political leaders.

The importance of Rand's thought

In addition to her novels and plays, Rand wrote non-fiction on *philosophy* – the study of reality and existence, how we know and understand the world, and what that implies for morality and politics.

Reality and its implications

Her approach is interesting for many reasons, not least because she sees reality, knowledge, human nature, morality, politics, economics, and even art as all intimately connected. While many philosophers focus on just one element, to Rand they are integral parts of an overall system.

She called this system *Objectivism*. It starts with the idea that there is a real world outside us that would continue to exist even without us. We can get to know the nature and workings of this world, but only if we think *objectively*. That means starting with the raw facts of our perceptions and using reason to understand them and build a coherent worldview upon them.

If we know how the world works, thought Rand, we can work out how we should best behave to thrive in it. That gives us a new way to determine what is morally right or wrong, and politically workable or unworkable – not on the traditional basis of religion, emotion, or authority, but on the *objective* basis of *reason*.

Reality and morality

This is a remarkable claim, and given the controversial nature of the moral principles and political institutions that Rand says are implied by this reasoning process, one can see why it draws criticism. In politics, she believes that reason prescribes freedom and capitalism, while the moral code that our reason dictates is not altruism and self-sacrifice – as so many moralists teach – but *rational self-interest.*

These, says Rand, are what guide us toward life, prosperity, the achievement of our values, and happiness. By contrast, the traditional morality of altruism and self-sacrifice does huge damage: success is decried and exploited, while failure and incapacity are rewarded – a one-way ticket, she says, to decline, dispute, and destruction. Having lived in Soviet Russia, she perhaps understood such problems better than most.

Whether or not you accept the view that morality can be based objectively on fact, Rand's approach remains an important critique of common political and moral ideas, such as Marxism and religion. To her, it is reason and knowledge that create value – physical labor, as Marx would have it. And religious faith cannot move mountains, never mind grow food and heal the sick. That takes technology, which in turn requires creative minds.

A new defense of liberty

But to work, creative minds must be free – to interact with the world, to reason, to learn, and to identify and serve our needs and values. The process cannot be forced. Liberty, to Rand, is therefore essential to human survival and progress.

This is a new and forceful defense of liberty, one based on what Rand saw as an objective understanding of our species and our world, not on personal, subjective opinions and conventions.

Our political and economic arrangements, likewise, must be based in liberty. The only economic system that is compatible with complete freedom, says Rand, is laissez-faire capitalism. And that depends on the existence of private property and a rule of law by which people can trade confidently without being coerced. The role of the state is merely to keep everyone to these rules and suppress violence; no other state activity can be justified.

Critics and adherents

Rand's confidence in our ability to know an external world is controversial among philosophers. Many skeptics suggest that our experiences may be just a dream, or an illusion, or at best a distortion of reality. Other critics doubt that even reliable knowledge of reality can be any guide to our moral or political actions.

Rand's moral idea that we should reject altruism and value things in terms of our own interest is corrupting, say critics. It ignores the fine, but crucial, lines between self-esteem and conceit, self-interest and greed, integrity and vanity. It is at odds with nature, since we are a social species and are naturally disposed to care for others, even strangers. Can all the world's religions be wrong in promoting altruism? And, of course, Rand's political conclusions – freedom, private property, and a minimal state – are equally unpopular among academics.

But academic opposition does not mean that Rand's ideas can be dismissed. On the contrary, they deserve to be taken seriously – if for no other reason than the fact that they have attracted so many adherents from all walks of life.

3 RAND'S LIFE AND WRITINGS

Turbulent childhood in Russia

Ayn Rand was born Alisa Zinov'yevna Rosenbaum in 1905, the first of three daughters of a middle-class Russian-Jewish family in St Petersburg. By age nine she had already decided to become a writer – inspired by the tale of the heroic British soldier Cyrus Paltons in a children's magazine. Later, after her mother took her to the cinema, she developed a passion for writing movie scenarios.

But in 1917, when she was just 12, Petrograd (as St Petersburg was then called) became the focus of the February and October Revolutions. When the Bolsheviks eventually won control, her father's pharmacy business and the family home were confiscated.

To escape the conflict and the harsh conditions in the city – shockingly portrayed in Rand's semi-autobiographical novel *We the Living* (1936) – the family moved to Crimea. Her father started a new pharmacy business, but that again was nationalized when the Red Army arrived. So when Alisa completed high school in 1921, they returned to Petrograd.

She was one of the first women to enroll in the State University. American history and politics, and Western plays, music, and cinema particularly enthused her. In addition to the novelists Fyodor Dostoevsky and Victor Hugo that she had read in Crimea, she now discovered other thinkers who would influence her later career, such as the Greek philosopher Aristotle.

But (again like the heroine Kira in *We the Living*) she was dismayed by how the communists suppressed free thought and free speech. Together with other 'bourgeois' students, she was purged from the university, but after foreign academics protested, she eventually graduated in 1924.

In these dark times, she became increasingly absorbed by Western plays, operettas, and films. Determined to become a screenwriter, she entered the state Cinematic Institute in Leningrad (as the Soviets had renamed the city), where she chose her professional name of Ayn Rand. She knew that she had no future in a stifling communist Russia and yearned to be part of the can-do culture portrayed in American movies. She obtained a visa to visit relatives in Chicago. Her parents helped to pay the passage. But she had no intention of returning.

New career in America

Landing in New York in 1926, Rand was overwhelmed by the impressive (and, to her, heroic) winter skyline. She went on to Chicago, where one of her relatives owned a cinema, allowing her to indulge her passion for films. She extended her visa and, with a borrowed $100 and a letter of recommendation from a film-distributor friend of her relatives, set out for California.

On her second day in Hollywood, a chance meeting with the leading filmmaker Cecil B. DeMille – who saw her staring at him as he left the studios – led him to hire her as an extra in the religious film *King of Kings*. Two weeks later she met the young actor Frank O'Connor, whom she married in 1929, just before her visa ran out. She became a US citizen in 1931.

Rand reviewed scripts for DeMille, then worked in the RKO Pictures wardrobe department while developing her own writing skills. In 1932 she sold her first screenplay, *Red Pawn*, a spy drama set on a Russian prison island, to Universal Studios. Her courtroom-drama stage play *Night of January 16th* (in which members of the audience act as the jury) was produced in Hollywood in 1934 and on Broadway in 1935. She was becoming a successful writer. To further her career, and anticipating the Broadway run, she and Frank moved to New York in late 1934.

She finished her novel *We the Living* in 1934, but its portrait of the brutal reality of life in the Soviet Union was at odds with the mood of the 'Red Decade,' in which Western intellectuals actively praised communism for its bold vision. Nor did the Russian idea of a 'philosophical novel' fit well with American culture. The book was eventually published in 1936 to disappointing reviews, though it fared better outside the US (and, without Rand's knowledge, was turned into two films in Italy). For the same reasons, it was her UK publisher who in 1938 first released her next book, *Anthem*, a novella set in a dystopian future where the idea of individuality has been extinguished.

Breakthrough novel

Nevertheless, she received crucial encouragement from Isabel Paterson, the influential *New York Herald Tribune* literary columnist and prominent libertarian thinker, who exchanged ideas with her and assured Rand of her originality.

Her breakthrough novel, *The Fountainhead*, appeared in 1943. Reactions were mixed. Critics scorned its 700-page length or saw its characters as unsympathetic loudspeakers for the author's views. But reader-to-reader recommendation made *The Fountainhead* a major literary success, and by 1945 it ranked sixth on the *New York Times* bestseller list.

Like *We the Living*, its theme is individualism versus collectivism – this time in the realm of creativity rather than politics. A philosophical romance, its plot centers around Howard Roark, a principled, uncompromising, and visionary modern architect – Rand's first personification of her ideal man – and heroine Dominique Francon, who shares his values but has withdrawn from what she sees as a contemptibly mediocre world.

The Fountainhead made Rand famous as a champion of individualism. One of those who read and admired it was the leading actor Gary Cooper, who offered Warner Bros. his services to play Roark for a screen version. Rand agreed to return from New York to Hollywood to write the script, but on condition that the studio did not change a word of it – a condition that, despite arguments, was honored.

When the film appeared in 1949, critics again saw the characters more as philosophical mouthpieces than as real human beings. The film was not a commercial success.

But it attracted a big following, which boosted sales of the book, and brought Rand considerable wealth – allowing her and Frank to buy a large (and, appropriately, modernist) ranch house in California.

Atlas Shrugged

Rand actively opposed the spread of communist sympathies in Hollywood. Her *Screen Guide for Americans* explained how filmmakers could spot and resist communist propaganda in their scripts. In 1947 she appeared as a friendly witness before the House Un-American Activities Committee. It all deepened the hostility against her from the left-leaning intellectuals who dominated cinema, literature, and criticism.

But by then, she had already begun work on a new novel, *Atlas Shrugged*. To complete it, she returned to New York, where a group of admirers – ironically dubbed 'The Collective' – gathered around her.

The 1,200-page *Atlas Shrugged* was published in 1957. Its themes, said Rand, were 'the role of the mind in man's existence' and her new morality of *rational self-interest*. It portrays a crumbling economy in which creative people reject their exploitation by others and withdraw to found their own society based on *egoism* – the refusal to live for the sake of others or to expect others to live for you. Like *The Fountainhead*, the plot involves a love affair, between the capable railroad boss Dagny Taggart and the innovative steelmaker Hank Rearden – and then with the mastermind behind the strike, John Galt.

The critics scorned the novel's polemical tone, its politics, and its length. But millions of readers found the book, its story, and its characters compelling – and still do. It soon peaked at third place on the *New York Times* bestseller list and went on to become one of the world's most influential books. Today it continues to sell tens of thousands of copies a year.

The Objectivist movement and its discontents

Rand's fame now brought her invitations to lecture to colleges and other groups and to appear on TV talk shows – where her direct style and evident passion for her unconventional views won over audiences.

From 1962, she established and wrote for a periodical, *The Objectivist Newsletter*, which morphed into a larger journal, *The Objectivist*, and from 1971 became *The Ayn Rand Letter*. Many of her essays for these journals were collected into a stream of non-fiction books including *The Virtue of Selfishness* (1964), on morality; *Capitalism: The Unknown Ideal* (1966), on economics and politics; *The Romantic Manifesto* (1969), on art and literature; and *Introduction to Objectivist Epistemology* (1979), on how we form concepts.

One of Rand's early followers was Nathan Blumenthal, who as a teenager sought her out. Changing his name to Nathaniel Branden, he worked closely with Rand on issues in philosophy and psychology, ran the newsletter with her, and grew the network of followers. With her approval he created the Nathaniel Branden Institute, making a business out of promoting and debating her ideas. Rand herself became a popular and charismatic speaker at the institute's events and on college campuses.

Rand admired Branden's intellect and drive. In 1954 they realized they had romantic feelings for each other (though he was much younger and recently married). To Branden's surprise, she persuaded their respective spouses to indulge an affair; they met regularly at Rand's apartment.

In 1968, though their romantic feelings had cooled, Rand discovered that Branden was having yet another affair. There was a spectacular split between them, abruptly ending their personal and professional links. In a lengthy article in *The Objectivist*, Rand accused Branden of abusing her trust, exploiting her name, defaulting on his promises, and departing from her principles. In reply, he upbraided her followers for treating the charismatic Rand as infallible and for judging people by their loyalty to her.

Rand completely eliminated Branden from her life and work. He was shunned by the movement that he had helped to form around her – reinforcing the image of it as a 'Randroid' cult. Such animosities grew into deep divisions, echoes of which still linger in the Objectivist movement.

Final years

Rand continued giving talks to students, taking controversial stances on many issues, including education, student protests, abortion, the Vietnam War, the military draft, the Arab-Israeli War, anti-monopoly laws, and much else.

But in the 1970s various personal events distracted Rand from her work. Though the Iron Curtain had long prevented communication with her Russian family, she at last made contact with her sister Nora, who visited her in New York. Sadly the visit caused only distress. Time and events had created unbridgeable distances between them, and after a short stay Nora returned to the Soviet Union.

Soon after, Rand – a lifetime smoker – underwent lung cancer surgery. Her husband Frank was also in failing health. She ended her newsletter writing and undertook fewer public appearances.

'I have lost my greatest value,' she remarked when Frank died in 1979. Though she rallied to work on the script for a TV mini-series based on *Atlas Shrugged*, she did not live to complete it. In 1982, returning from a speaking event in New Orleans – to her delight, and redolent of *Atlas Shrugged*, the organizer had sent her a private train – she fell ill, and died soon afterward at her New York apartment. Over her coffin was placed a giant dollar sign – her symbol for 'a free country – for achievement, for success, for ability, for man's creative power.'

Continuing influence

After her death, Rand's close intellectual colleague (and legal executor and heir) Leonard Peikoff established the Ayn Rand Institute to promote her ideas. Differences about Objectivism and how closely it should stick to Rand's views led Peikoff's student and associate David Kelley to create a rival body, the Institute for Objectivist Studies (later called the Objectivist Center, and then the Atlas Society).

Today, Objectivist groups have been established on four different continents, while the Anthem Foundation for Objectivist Scholarship, created in 2001, sponsors professors at various US colleges.

Through these and other sources, Rand's philosophy is now getting serious critical appraisal in academic journals and books.

Meanwhile, more of Rand's output has been published, including books based on her correspondence, journals, essays, interviews, and speeches. The Italian films were re-released as *We the Living*; the play *Ideal* was staged; the novella *Anthem* was adapted into a stage play; various scripts and short stories have emerged. There was even a Bollywood version of *Night of January 16th*.

Also, biographies and memoirs have appeared. These include a book by Nathaniel Branden, another by his wife Barbara that was made into a TV movie, and the Oscar-nominated film *Ayn Rand: A Sense of Life*.

Today, Rand is a central (if still controversial) part of popular culture. In 1999, her image appeared on a US postal stamp. *Atlas Shrugged* reached top place on Amazon.com's bestselling fiction list after the 2008 crash, amid fears of an economic meltdown resonant of the crisis depicted in the novel. People evidently still turn to Rand for answers, and for strength.

A timeline of Rand's life and work

1905   Born Alisa Zinov'yevna Rosenbaum in St Petersburg, Russia

1914   Makes it her ambition to become a writer

1917   The storming of the Winter Palace in Petrograd (formerly St Petersburg) begins the communist revolution

1918   Moves with her family to Crimea to escape civil war

1921   Returns with her family to Petrograd; enters Petrograd State University

1924   Eventually allowed to graduate after foreign scientists' complaints against purges of 'bourgeois' students

1924   Enrols in the state Cinematic Institute; chooses the professional name of Ayn Rand

1925   Her first publication appears, a short monograph on femme fatale actress Pola Negri

1925   Obtains a visa to visit US relatives

1926   Arrives in New York, stays six months with Chicago relatives, goes to Hollywood and is hired by Cecil B. DeMille as an extra

1927   Employed by DeMille as a junior screen writer

1929   Marries actor Frank O'Connor; becomes a US resident

1931   Becomes a US citizen

1932   Sells her first screenplay, spy thriller *Red Pawn*, to Universal Studios for $1,500, though it is never produced

1934	Writes the novelette *Ideal*, but it is not published until 2015
1934	Her first play, courtroom drama *Woman on Trial*, produced in Hollywood
1934	*Woman on Trial* moves to Broadway as *Night of January 16th*, and runs for seven months
1935	Begins work on a new novel, *The Fountainhead*
1936	Publishes the semi-autobiographical novel *We the Living*, set in Soviet Russia
1936	Revises *Ideal* into a stage play, though it is not produced until 1989
1938	Publishes the novella *Anthem* in the United Kingdom, having failed to find a sympathetic US publisher
1939	Writes the philosophical murder mystery play *Think Twice*, though it is never produced during her lifetime.
1940	Becomes a volunteer for the presidential campaign of Wendell Willkie (Republican)
1940	*The Unconquered*, her stage adaptation of *We the Living*, is produced on Broadway but is not a success
1941	Paramount produces a film based on *Night of January 16th*
1942	*We the Living* made into Italian films *Noi Vivi* and *Addio, Kira*
1943	*The Fountainhead* published
1943	Sells *The Fountainhead* film rights to Warner Bros.
1943	Hired by producer Hal Willis as screenwriter and script editor

1944   Publishes 'The Only Path to Tomorrow,' a pilot article for a never-completed book, *The Moral Basis of Individualism*

1945   Two years after publication, *The Fountainhead* reaches number 6 on the *New York Times* bestseller list

1945   *Love Letters*, adapted by Rand from a Christopher Massie novel, gets bad reviews but is a box-office success

1945   *You Came Along*, a comedy-romance with a screenplay largely re-written by Rand, is released to broadly positive reviews

1946   Revised version of *Anthem* finally published in the US

1947   Begins drafting *Atlas Shrugged*

1947   Testifies as a 'friendly witness' to the US House Un-American Activities Committee

1949   Film version of *The Fountainhead*, starring Gary Cooper, is released after many delays

1950   Meets admirer Nathan Blumenthal (later Nathaniel Branden), who would become her promoter and associate

1951   Moves back to New York where a discussion group of admirers, jokingly called 'The Collective,' forms around her

1954   Begins an affair with Nathaniel Branden

1957   *Atlas Shrugged* is published and reaches number 3 on the *New York Times* bestseller list

1958   Branden creates the Nathaniel Branden Lectures, later the Nathaniel Branden Institute (NBI)

1959   Revised edition of *We the Living* published

1960s–70s Undertakes lecture tours on Objectivism

1961   *For the New Intellectual* published

1962   *The Objectivist Newsletter* appears

1962   Nathaniel and Barbara Branden publish *Who Is Ayn Rand?* on Rand's life, ethics, psychology, and fiction

1963   Receives honorary degree from Lewis & Clark College

1964   Endorses Republican presidential hopeful Barry Goldwater

1964   *The Virtue of Selfishness* published

1966   *Capitalism: The Unknown Ideal* published

1966   *The Objectivist Newsletter* expands and is renamed *The Objectivist*

1966–67   *The Objectivist* serializes Rand's main philo-sophical treatise, *Introduction to Objectivist Epistemology*

1967   Appears on American TV show *The Tonight Show*

1968   Relationship with Branden and the NBI ends abruptly; she scorns his actions at length in *The Objectivist*

1969   *The Romantic Manifesto* is published, encapsulat-ing Rand's views on art and literature

1971   *The New Left: The Anti-Industrial Revolution* published

1974   Undergoes lung cancer surgery after years of heavy smoking

1976   Endorses Leonard Peikoff's lectures on Objectiv-ism as the best exposition of her philosophy

1976	Stops writing for *The Objectivist*
1979	Husband Frank O'Connor dies
1979	*Introduction to Objectivist Epistemology* re-published, with an additional 1967 essay by Leonard Peikoff
1982	Publication of *Philosophy: Who Needs It*
1982	Calls Peikoff's *The Ominous Parallels* 'The first book by an Objectivist philosopher other than myself'
1982	Dies of heart failure at her New York apartment; a large floral dollar sign is placed on her coffin
1984	Douglas Den Uyl and Douglas Rasmussen publish a critical academic appraisal, *The Philosophic Thought of Ayn Rand*
1985	Leonard Peikoff and Ed Snider found the Ayn Rand Institute
1986	Re-edited version of Italian films released as *We the Living*
1986	Publication of Barbara Branden's *The Passion of Ayn Rand*, focusing on Rand's personal life
1987	Former Collective member Alan Greenspan becomes chairman of the US Federal Reserve
1987	Foundation of the Ayn Rand Society, a professional group of scholars within the American Philosophical Society
1989	Rand's play *Ideal* is produced for the first time
1989	*Gawaahi* [Evidence], a Bollywood version of *Night of January 16th*, is released
1989	Nathaniel Branden publishes *Judgment Day: My Years with Ayn Rand*

1990   David Kelley founds the Institute for Objectivist
        Studies (later the Objectivist Center, then the
        Atlas Society)

1991   A Library of Congress survey reports *Atlas
        Shrugged* the second-most influential book in
        America (after the Bible)

1991   Leonard Peikoff publishes *Objectivism: The Philos-
        ophy of Ayn Rand*, a 'comprehensive statement' of
        Rand's worldview

1995   Much of Rand's correspondence is published as
        Letters of Ayn Rand

1996   Release of *Ayn Rand: A Sense of Life*, Michael Pax-
        ton's documentary film on Rand's life and ideas

1999   Release of TV film *The Passion of Ayn Rand*, based
        on Barbara Branden's account of Rand's affair
        with Nathaniel Branden

1999   First issue of *The Journal of Ayn Rand Studies*
        appears

1999   Rand's image appears on a US postage stamp

2000   Edited transcripts of Rand's talks on fiction-writ-
        ing are published as *The Art of Fiction*

2001   Rand's 1958 lectures on nonfiction are published
        as *The Art of Nonfiction*

2001   Entrepreneur (and later, historian) John McCaskey
        creates the Anthem Foundation for Objectivist
        Scholarship

2009   Following the financial crisis, *Atlas Shrugged* is
        ranked number 1 on Amazon.com's bestselling
        fiction list

2009   Publication of *Ayn Rand and the World She Made*, a biography by journalist Anne C. Heller

2009   Publication of *Goddess of the Market* by historian Jennifer Burns, exploring Rand's influence on political movements

2011   First part of a three-part film adaptation of *Atlas Shrugged* is produced (subsequent parts appear in 2012 and 2014)

2012   The Adam Smith Institute think tank hosts the first annual *Ayn Rand Lecture* in London

2013   Rand's novel *Anthem* adapted into a stage play

2014   Scripts of *The Unconquered* published

2014   Foundation of the Ayn Rand Institute Europe

2015   Rand's novelette *Ideal* is published

2016   Publication of *A Companion to Ayn Rand*, edited by American scholars Allan Gotthelf and Gregory Salmieri

4 OUTLINE OF RAND'S WORLDVIEW

At a sales conference for *Atlas Shrugged*, Rand was asked whether she could explain her philosophy – how she understood the world and humanity – while standing on one leg. She did so, in 10 words:

'Metaphysics [i.e. the nature of the universe] – Objective Reality;
Epistemology [i.e. how we can know about the universe] – Reason;
Ethics [i.e. the moral principles by which we should live] – Self-Interest;
Politics [i.e. the principles of social organization] – Capitalism.'

She had not yet written in depth on art but could have added:

'Aesthetics [i.e. the principles of art] – Romanticism.'

Those 12 words neatly summarize Rand's philosophy, which she called *Objectivism*. And philosophy, she maintained, is vital in all parts of human affairs. We cannot properly choose the political principles that will serve society well without rooting them in the moral principles that are right for individuals. In turn, those moral principles must be rooted a clear knowledge of the world and its workings. And to get that, we need to use a valid, logical method.

For us to thrive, therefore, we must conduct every part of our lives *objectively* – to live on the basis of reality as properly understood through reason and logic. We cannot expect to prosper by following our whim or prejudice or wishful thinking. We must *choose* to accept reality and to think rationally and objectively.

Rand on reality

The metaphysics Rand talks of is our search to discover the ultimate nature of reality, of things, and of existence. What kind of a world do we live in? Is it real or merely an illusion? Is it natural, or is it controlled by something supernatural?

Rand insists that the world is real and natural. There are solid things around us, which – quite automatically – we are aware of. And we are also aware that these things exist, and continue to exist, whether we are around or not. They do not just disappear when we shut our eyes. In other words, *existence* itself is something real – or, as Rand puts it, 'existence exists.'

Our world, she concludes, is not a dream, nor something magical, nor illogical, nor arbitrary. Things exist, and have settled relationships to each other, without contradictions: we are surrounded both by solid things, and solid facts.

Rand on human knowledge

The question for *epistemology*, the theory of knowledge, is how we get reliable knowledge of this world. This is not about *what* we know – that is science – but *how* we know it. And that, she thinks, hinges on both reality and ourselves.

Our brains automatically make us aware that things exist, that things *are*, she explains. But to survive and flourish, we also need to learn *what* those things are. That, however, is not automatic: we are not born knowing what everything is. We have to learn it, which requires deliberate thought and effort. We must choose to focus our minds on the problem, work out what things are, and check that our method and conclusions are valid.

It is this deliberate use of *reason*, says Rand, which builds knowledge upon the foundation of our awareness. Reason is the uniquely human faculty by which we identify things – separating and filing them into different categories, such as 'humans,' 'animals,' or 'trees' – on the basis of their essential distinguishing features. And through logic, we ensure that the filing categories – or concepts – that we form are consistent and not contradictory.

Rand believes that this unique faculty explains human success. It enables us to file, manage, and use a vast amount of information about the world. It allows us to distill a huge number of observations into a single idea. That enables us to think about highly abstract concepts, such as 'freedom' or 'business' or 'prosperity' – and about the relationships between them. This helps us survive and flourish.

Rand on morality

Ethics, the study of how we form moral judgments, tackles the abstract concept of 'good.' We are not born knowing what is good or evil, says Rand: we must learn it. Fortunately, just as we can learn the nature of existence by using our reason, we can learn the principles of morality by the same method.

The key to understanding moral values, she argues, is life. The reason living things have values and lifeless things do not is that we face choices that make a difference to us. Our comfort, safety, health – and ultimately our own survival, to which all these values contribute – depend on what we do.

Rand concludes that the measure or *standard* of value is life. And for each of us, our moral purpose is our own life.

The traditional morality of self-sacrifice – altruism – is destructive, she warns. Self-sacrifice harms your own life, while the self-sacrifice of others encourages you to live as a parasite. Neither is sustainable; altruism cannot be a virtue. Instead, you should value yourself, act in your own long-term rational interest, and fight for your own values. The reward of *that* morality, she says, is life, happiness, and self-esteem.

Rand on politics and economics

Rand argues that the values and principles of social organization – *politics* – follow logically from the ethics that guide our individual actions (which in turn depends on how we understand reality). Philosophy guides the course of nations, just as much as it guides each one of us.

What links individual and social actions, says Rand, are rights – moral principles about when individuals are free to act without others restricting that freedom. And since our standard of value is life, she continues, the most basic right is our right to life. From that, all other rights follow.

For example, if we are to survive and live as complete human beings, we must use and act on our reason. So the right to life implies the right to think, to work productively, and to keep the fruits of our efforts – that is, the property that we create. The only system that guarantees all that, Rand maintains, is unregulated laissez-faire capitalism.

It is certainly possible for people to violate our rights through force. But that is evil, says Rand, because it makes us act against our own reason, knowledge, and values. Force must therefore be countered. Unfortunately we cannot rely on individuals to retaliate rationally and proportionately. So we need an agency – government – that can protect our rights by taking measured action against those who initiate force. It is no small function, requiring a justice system with law, police, courts, and punishments. But the defense of individual rights is the sole function of government. Nothing more can be justified, unless everyone agrees.

Rand on art and literature

Rand sees *aesthetics* – the principles of art – as yet another branch of philosophy. While ethics examines how we can do what is good, aesthetics examines how art communicates what is important. Once again, it is not a matter of whim or mystery, but a rational process.

Rand explains that true artists – including painters, sculptors, authors, and dramatists – focus our attention by selecting and representing the things they see as important and omitting what they see as trivial or incidental. In this way, they recreate reality, giving us a high-relief version that helps us sharpen our understanding of existence.

Art can communicate abstract concepts by expressing them in a physical form that we can grasp directly. It can teach us something about the world and how it works. That is why we need art. And we can evaluate an artwork on these aesthetic principles, even if we dislike it or disagree with what it is saying.

Rand's image of a heroic being

The heroes of Rand's fiction reflect her own moral ideal. They are individualists, relying on their own values, judgments, and efforts. They expect nothing free from others and recognize nobody's right to take from them. They have a strong sense of their own moral worth and the worth of those who genuinely earn respect. They despise parasites. They are intelligent, rational, creative, visionary, resolute, and confident. They take pride in their achievements and integrity.

The antagonists in Rand's novels do not live by reason. They include bullies who use force or government power to exploit the creative thinkers, parasites who feed off the achievers, mediocrities who cannot think for themselves and conformists who cannot be bothered to, manipulators who want to make others supine to their wishes, and those who simply hate others for their success.

Such is the barometer that Rand holds up against the values of our culture. In her fiction, as in her other writing, she makes plain her belief that ultimately only a culture of reason can endure.

5 RAND ON THE NATURE OF REALITY

To Rand, our worldview – our *philosophy* – influences every part of our conduct. In order to prosper in our personal, social, political, and economic activities, we need a clear understanding of the world and of human nature.

Metaphysics, the study of the fundamental nature of reality and existence, is a good place to start. Though many philosophers have questioned whether the world we experience could be a dream, a distortion, an illusion, or a mere shadow of some deeper reality, Rand takes a commonsense view. The world that we are aware of, she insists, *is* reality. The challenge is to understand it.

We are automatically aware that things exist: we can see and touch them. But while such sensations and perceptions tell us that things exist, they do not tell us what they are. If we are to survive and thrive, this is something we must work out. And when we apply our reason to this problem, we discover that the world is no mystery or illusion, but a reality of solid things and solid facts. *That* is the reality in which our lives and activities must be grounded.

Basic axioms

To show why, Rand starts with three *axioms* – statements of facts that, she claims, are self-evidently true.

First, we know that things exist. Our brains make us aware of them. We might not know their exact nature – exactly what they are and how they behave – but we know they are there. And we know that they do not just vanish when we are not looking. They have an existence of their own. Or as Rand puts it, 'existence exists' too.

Second, we are aware that things exist. We perceive them. We are conscious of them. That means that we must exist, and our consciousness exists. The fact that we are conscious also implies that things do exist. We cannot be conscious of nothing; we have to be conscious of something.

Third, to be something implies that a thing must have *identity* – a collection of attributes that distinguish it as a particular thing and not something else. As Rand puts it, 'existence is identity' or 'A is A' – one cannot separate a thing's existence (*that* it is) from its essence (*what* it is). A thing has to be something, and it cannot be something else at the same time. That is the *law of identity*.

Existence, consciousness, and identity are therefore all intertwined. And they are self-evident: they require no proof beyond what we experience. Indeed, says Rand, to disprove them, you would have to assume them: you cannot frame any argument without referring to things and your awareness of them. These axioms are therefore the foundations of all our knowledge and reasoning.

Identity and causality

Perception, which tells us that things are – that they exist – is automatic. But the way we come to understand what things are, and how they behave, is through reason. That is not automatic. It requires a choice. It requires us to think and think objectively.

To explain the process, Rand imagines how a child learns to view the world. At first, the child senses only a confusion of separate colors, noises, smells, tastes, and other sensations. But a child's brain automatically connects these into groups of sensations – perceptions – that give it the ability to be aware of things, not just of individual and seemingly random sensations. So instead of seeing only disparate patches of color and shape, for example, the child sees a whole thing, a whole entity, such as a particular table.

Further on in this process, the child observes the attributes, scale, actions, and relationships of these entities and comes to realize that they behave, and affect the child, in different but consistent ways. A table, for example, is hard to the touch, but a teddy bear is soft. A dog moves and barks, but a table does not. A table can squash a teddy bear, but teddy bears do not squash tables. How things behave and affect other things – *causality* – is also a part of their identity. Causality, as Rand puts it, is the law of identity applied to action.

Existence and consciousness

The child notices something else too. Close your eyes, and things seem to disappear; open your eyes, and you see they are still there, unchanged. In such a way we become aware of existence and of our own consciousness. We become aware that things have an existence of their own, independent of us. We cannot change existence by closing our eyes or wishing things away.

That, declares Rand, is why it does us no good merely to wish that things were different or pray for them to change or hope that they will go away if we ignore them. Things remain, inescapably, what they are. They continue to exist and to behave according to their fundamental nature, whatever our particular desires and dreams might be. Or as she puts it, existence has primacy over consciousness.

In other words, we cannot claim to know the world by looking inward at our feelings; we have to look outward to the hard facts of reality. The world is not a figment of our imagination, says Rand, nor something we can create and change at will. It is a given and it must be respected as such.

Necessity and choice

There is no alternative to accepting the metaphysically given, as she calls it. Facts are facts: things are what they are, and exist and behave according to their nature, regardless of us. They are necessary – parts of an inescapable reality.

The only non-necessary things in our world are the things that we human beings, by our own free will, choose to do or to make. But even then, our choices are still limited by the given facts of reality. We cannot choose to make things what they are not, for example, nor to change events just by wishing it. We can certainly rearrange things that already exist – making clay and straw into bricks, say – but we cannot create things out of nothing.

Whatever we choose to do, we simply have to accept the facts of nature. There is no point in denying them or blaming them for our failures: they are simply given. But the facts that result from our choices are *not* given. They can be judged good or bad – and they must be, if we are to choose wisely in the future.

The rejection of reality

Overlooking this difference leads to deep mistakes. For a start, complains Rand, many people assume that the products of human choice – the political culture, for example – cannot be changed. So they get sucked into mindless conformity, following the norm, the mob, or the dictator.

Others, known as *idealists*, like the Ancient Greek philosopher Plato, imagine that the world is controlled by (or is a mere shadow of) something supernatural. This leads some to believe that we can change reality through our feelings or wishes or prayers. But this is fantasy, complains Rand. It presumes that consciousness (or 'spirit') is primary. It ignores the basic axioms of reality. And because it is not based on reason, it leads to contradictions.

Equally, there are the *materialists*, such as the German political thinker Karl Marx and the American 'behaviorist' psychologist B. F. Skinner, who accept *facts* but deny the role of consciousness, seeing it as either a mystical fiction, or a mere by-product of physical brain activity. But, argues Rand, without awareness, without consciousness, we would have no grasp of reality at all.

It is not easy to get a valid grasp on reality. But we are greatly helped if we understand the process and method that we must adopt to do so. And this is the second strand of Rand's philosophy.

6 HOW WE UNDERSTAND THE WORLD

This second strand is *epistemology* – the question of how we gain knowledge and understanding of reality. Not *what* we know (again, that is science), but *how* we know things.

The process of understanding

Raw data about the world, Rand explains, comes to us through our senses. Our brains automatically take that seemingly random stream of unrelated sensations and integrate them into coherent *perceptions*. These perceptions are what make us aware that things exist.

But understanding what those things *are* is not automatic. It requires an act of will from us – the deliberate application of mind and thought – to turn raw perceptions *of* things into useful knowledge *about* things. This deliberate process is what Rand calls *reason*.

Reason involves consciously integrating our perceptions into mental groupings that we call *concepts*. It is by developing, refining, and testing our concepts that we grasp the true nature of things. That takes focus and effort. We are not born with a mind full of good concepts that truly reflect reality. We need to learn and follow rules of sound thinking if we are to create them. We need to keep our thinking objective and not distorted by our prejudices, dreams, or whims.

The validity of the senses

Some doubters claim that Rand's argument falls at the first fence. We can never have valid knowledge of the world, they say, because our senses may distort the reality they transmit to us. But to Rand, our perceptions are perfectly valid. The only job our senses have to do is to make us aware that something exists. Then it is up to our reason to understand exactly what exists.

Reality and awareness are intimately entwined. Our sensations stem partly from the nature of real objects and partly from the nature of our own sense organs. We may experience reality differently – as normal and color-blind people do – but it is the same reality, says Rand, as reason can demonstrate to us.

Color, taste, and so on are not just 'in the mind,' somehow independent of any real objects. Nor are they qualities of objects, somehow independent of us. Rather, they are the effects that objects have on us. And that is how we perceive reality. There is no distortion: the object and our senses are both part of our perception. The only place where mistakes and distortions can occur is when we consciously start thinking about what those perceptions really represent.

The early stages of consciousness

There are several stages to the process. As already outlined, very young children at first experience only seemingly random, isolated sensations. Later, our young brains automatically integrate these sensations into perceptions. So instead of sensing a vast buzz of green and brown shapes, for example, we now perceive a coherent group of sensations (a *percept*), which an adult would call a 'tree.'

We are now aware of a thing, an entity, something different from our other background sensations and indeed from other entities. At first, every percept – each individual 'tree' that we perceive – seems unique. But again our young brains automatically start to grasp the differences, similarities, and relationships between them. We come to see entities no longer as unique, but as members of a group of objects ('trees') that have unifying features.

Concept formation

So far, the process is automatic – in both humans and animals. But now, says Rand, we begin to do something uniquely human, and crucial to our human understanding and survival. After our brains have automatically isolated these percepts, and distinguished what makes them similar or different, we now apply our reason. We integrate them into new groups – into new mental entities, which we call *concepts*.

This takes conscious effort: it requires us to choose to think about the essential natures of different things. But by using concepts, we can process and use far more information about the world, and thereby boost our chances of surviving and thriving. If we see each tree only as a unique object, there is a limit to how many individual trees our minds can grasp. With the concept 'tree,' however, we can talk about *every* tree – not just the ones we can see, but any number of trees, wherever they happen to be, and whether in the past, present, or future.

We can go further, building up from these *existential* concepts that refer to solid objects, such as a 'tree,' to *abstract* concepts that exist *only* in our minds, such as 'trees' – or even higher abstractions still, such as 'vegetation' or 'life' or 'nature.'

This is a huge benefit to us because it enables us to act on the basis of something far more sophisticated than immediate sensations and perceptions. It means we can analyze, and plan, far beyond our own place and time. We can also begin to understand the causal connections between abstract – but vital – concepts, such as 'business' and 'wealth.'

Concepts, in other words, are a form of knowledge that helps us make decisions and plans and which therefore promotes our survival and prosperity.

An active process

Again, this is not an automatic process. It is an active process, a deliberate and conscious process of working out how we can mentally file our grasp of things in the most accurate and useful ways. To come up with valid concepts, Rand insists, requires effort, thought, philosophy, method, and focus. It is a voluntary mental process that we must choose to engage in.

It can be a long and difficult process too. It can involve us fashioning long chains of concepts – building existential concepts on percepts ('tree'), then abstract concepts on those concepts ('trees'), then even more abstract concepts ('vegetation') on those. The most highly abstract concepts (such as 'justice' or 'bravery' or 'friendship') involve abstracting from thousands of observations and from hundreds of other concepts. And the further from perception these abstract concepts get, the harder it is to get them right. A bad concept may mislead and distort our thinking on many more.

It is therefore vital that our concepts are fit for their purpose – which is to reveal the essential similarities and differences between things. We can develop good concepts that do this well, but we can also come up with bad concepts that miss the essential distinguishing features of things. That is particularly true for our most abstract concepts.

At every stage, then, we need good method. We need to check that our concepts are rooted in solid fact and always square with reality without any contradiction. Only then will we have the sound knowledge that we need in order to make rational choices and to act in our own long-term interests.

Language and identity

Rand argues that another human faculty – *language* – is instrumental in making our concepts, however abstract, mentally manageable. We give names to each concept, turning them into 'concretes' that our minds can deal with. These names identify our concepts: they are the 'labels' that summarize what is in each mental 'file.' This makes language an essential tool of concept formation – and therefore an essential part of how we think.

But giving concepts an identity can be difficult. For example, asks Rand, how do you define 'man'? Your definition must summarize all the essential features that differentiate a man from everything else. It must apply to *all* men – past, present, and future. The more abstract concepts are even harder to pin down.

Identifying what makes us human is particularly important to Rand, since human understanding and actions are her whole focus. Following Aristotle, she ventures the definition that we are rational animals. Other features may also distinguish us from animals – our opposable thumbs, for instance. But a definition, she insists, must focus on what is fundamental, not on incidentals. And to her, the most important characteristic that separates us from other animals is that we are rational. We have the faculty to identify and integrate perceptual data into knowledge.

Thought, reality, and logic

Again, such a definition encapsulates a vast number of past and present observations of human beings and their thoughts and actions. A word, Rand jokes, is worth a thousand pictures. But however abstract our concepts are (such as 'man,' 'culture,' 'success,' 'humanity'), they must reflect reality at every stage. Our definitions cannot be arbitrary labels that we make up as we choose. They must derive from real and necessary facts. They must be objective.

Our conceptual knowledge is hierarchical – we put mental file folders inside other mental file folders, with increasing levels of abstraction (say, from 'chair' through 'furniture,' 'household goods' to 'property') and increasing distance from our raw perceptions. So for our abstract concepts to be valid, we must be sure of the validity of each step that we made in establishing them, and we must be able to trace their roots back to the perceptual level.

The method by which we check whether our concepts correspond to reality is logic. The identities we establish, and the definitions we use to describe them, must not lead to contradictions. Logic is about establishing what our concepts and definitions imply and then amending them if contradictions arise. We must be able to trace a contradiction-free line of argument back to perceptual fact or to self-evident axioms. An all-too-common error, complains Rand, is to build our concepts blindly on past mistakes.

Knowledge and its critics

Many philosophers before Rand have suggested that there exists a reality independent of us and our minds, but which we can come to know. The list of these realists, as they are called, includes Aristotle, Thomas Aquinas, Francis Bacon, René Descartes, John Locke, and many others.

A key difference is that while most realists thought that the only link we have to reality is the questionable evidence of our senses, Rand is a realist about perception too. Our perceptions, she maintains, are not just an array of sense data that come through our (potentially unreliable) sense organs, but a direct awareness of things. Other thinkers such as Thomas Reid held roughly similar views, but they are a minority.

Another difference is that Rand is not a realist about abstract concepts, as many, like Plato and Aquinas, were. To her, we can perceive that a particular 'tree' exists, regardless of us. But 'trees' or 'vegetation' are not 'real' things that exist regardless of us. They are abstract ideas that we form in our minds and that exist only in our minds. They are the filing system we use to bring mental order to our perceptions.

But Rand sees the debate on reality and how we know it as more than just an argument between *realists*, who presume the existence of a real world, and *skeptics*, like the Scottish philosopher David Hume, who argue that we can never know any reality beyond our own sensations. Her distinctive view is that real things do exist, but we know that only through their effects on us and on how we think about them. Reality cannot be separated from our minds, nor can our minds make reality anything we choose. To survive and prosper we need to choose to think objectively about what we experience, using logic and reason to build a clear picture of the world that is rooted in fact.

The invalidity of agnosticism

Some people, observes Rand, reject objective methods and believe in God, or in reincarnation, or that the planets control our lives. Unless we can prove them wrong, they claim, we must admit the possibility that they are right. So at the very least, they argue, we must admit that we cannot be sure, and remain *agnostic*.

No, says Rand: we are under no obligation to disprove such claims, nor even to take them seriously as worthy of consideration and debate. The onus is always on the speakers to produce factual evidence to support their beliefs. If they cannot, we can dismiss their assertions as merely arbitrary – with no greater foundation in reality than any other random idea, however bizarre.

It is therefore illegitimate to pass the burden of proof onto critics or to claim that we have to accept uncertainty, she concludes. If we have engaged in a logical process built on solid evidence within the context of the available facts, there is no uncertainty, no cause for agnosticism.

Reason and emotion

Other critics maintain that our desires and emotions are what drive us and that reason merely shows us the best way to achieve our ends. 'Reason is ... only the slave of the passions,' as David Hume put it. But Rand sees this as completely backward. Thought guides emotion, she says, not the other way around.

Reason, she reminds us, is the faculty that identifies things and files them into concepts. Emotions are a product of this rational process. Emotion is our psychological response to something that we value in some way – such as good, bad, useful, or dangerous. But in order to know what something *means* to us, we must first know what it is. We must already have applied our reason: reason precedes our emotions. Emotions may be useful in other ways, but they cannot tell us what is true.

Rand's philosophical stance

Rand concludes that traditional philosophy is fatally flawed because it fails to grasp that knowledge is based on both reality and mind. To her, knowledge is an intimate partnership between the two. To emphasize that, she describes the process of how we acquire knowledge as *psycho-epistemology*.

Having the right philosophy, then, is crucial to how we understand the world and operate within it. And this is just as true of our moral actions as of any other.

7   RAND ON MORALITY

Thinking about moral values and actions is vitally important to human beings, says Rand, because – uniquely among living things – we have the ability to choose how we behave, how we treat others, and the virtues and ideals to which we aspire.

But if we are to make *good* moral choices, we first need to make another choice. We must choose to think objectively – that is, to use our reason and focus it on establishing the true nature of things, without drift or evasion. Rand described where she believed that process would lead us as pithily as she had summarized her philosophy in general:

'For what end should a man live? – Answer: *Life*.
By what basic principle should he act to achieve this end? – Answer: *Reason*.
Who should profit from his actions? – Answer: *Oneself*.'

Facts and values

For centuries, moral philosophers have struggled with the problem of how to prove that their moral judgments are valid. We can prove facts – what *is* – but how do we prove values – what *ought to be*? Usually they adopt one of two possible answers: either that religion, tradition, or some other authority tells us what values and actions are good or bad; or that good and bad, right and wrong, are merely matters of personal opinion.

Neither answer, complains Rand, is objective: each regards facts and logic as irrelevant. But moral values *are* objective, she insists. They *can* be derived logically from facts. Just as reason can show us the nature of reality, so can it show us the nature of good and evil. This pursuit – *ethics* – is a rational one: provided we choose to apply our minds, we can discover moral values through our reason.

And the key fact on which those moral values rest, she says, is life.

Life and objective value

A *value*, explains Rand, is something that living beings strive to gain (or keep). They may, for example, value comfort and security, and they act to secure these values by pursuing specific goals (such as food, water, and shelter). But all these goals and values serve one ultimate end: *self-preservation* – their life.

To Rand, therefore, the very concept of value rests on the existence of a *purposive actor* – one who faces an alternative that makes a difference to it (such as hunger or contentment, and ultimately life or death).

Lifeless things, by contrast, have no values. A stone, for example, has no purpose and no goals and is unable to take any action. But something that can act but cannot be *harmed* – like an indestructible robot, she suggests – has no values either. Nothing it does (or does not do) makes any difference to it: action yields it no value.

Moral standard

Animals, for their part, are guided by instinct to pursue things that are generally good for them. But we human beings are different. We can choose how we act. That gives us a powerful flexibility – though it means that we might also make bad choices that ultimately destroy us. This, says Rand, is why we need ethics. With our very existence at stake, we need something to navigate us toward our ultimate goal of life – our *own* life – and away from destructive errors.

To identify which actions will ultimately prove destructive, she continues, we have to use our reason. We must accept our nature as human beings and strive to know what generally promotes our survival – survival, that is, as whole, thinking, purposive, productive, virtuous beings.

On the basis of this understanding, we need to identify and adopt the sort of life and values that a human being needs to survive and prosper – a *moral code* that will help us choose the specific actions that will promote this end.

To Rand, therefore, life is the ultimate standard of value – the principle against which our individual choices can be measured and judged good or evil. What furthers life is good; what threatens it is evil. Those who believe that moral values are merely a matter of personal choice, or are laid down by God or some other authority, get ethics quite wrong, because they miss the fact that moral values have a function – the objective *function* of preserving life.

The concept of objective value

Given this objective nature of morality, says Rand, we can have moral knowledge exactly like our other sorts of knowledge: a mental filing system, grounded in fact and developed by our reason, which helps us to understand, make sound choices, and survive. Like any other concepts, moral ideas like good, bad, right, wrong, just, or unjust are mental abstractions that allow us to process a vast amount of experience and thereby choose the values, goals, and actions that enable us to thrive. Ethics, therefore, is not something mystical or arbitrary, but an essential tool for survival. Ethics is the science of self-preservation.

And again, just as we have no inborn guide to what is, so we have no inborn guide to what ought to be. We must discover it by applying our minds objectively. Starting with facts and applying sound methods, we must work out whether it is right to tell a lie, for example, or good to give to the poor, or just to take up arms.

Reason, concludes Rand, is what makes all human value achievable. And the greatest *virtue* – the voluntary action by which we secure a value – is our use of reason. The greatest vice, likewise, is to reject reason: to refuse to think, to lose focus, to evade contradictions, to ignore (like an addict) the consequences of our actions, to hope that things will work out 'somehow.' If we are to choose life, we must accept reality.

The science of self-preservation

Reality, though, confronts individuals in terms of their own life or death. Every individual's ultimate goal is *self*-preservation. We must each choose our values and actions, says Rand, against the moral standard of our own life.

Her controversial conclusion, therefore, is that our main moral obligation is *self-interest* – to focus on our own survival and welfare. This she calls *egoism*.

Rand's egoism is not what people commonly call *self-ishness* (though to rouse readers from their altruism, she mischievously equated the two in her book title *The Virtue of Selfishness*). Egoism is not about selfishly robbing, defrauding, injuring, or even ignoring others. That is not ultimately compatible with our long-term, rational self-interest; to survive as whole human beings we need the cooperation and expertise of others, and those would not be good ways to get it. Nor should egoism be confused with *hedonism* – pursuing immediate pleasure with no thought to the consequences. Egoism focuses on the long-term requirements of human life.

Dealing with others

Egoists may be self-interested, but that does not mean there is constant conflict between them. Rational people realize that conflict is destructive.

Nor do we have to fight or rob others to gain from them. We can *trade* with them – freely and mutually giving up something of ours in exchange for something of theirs that we value more. That makes each of us better off.

And we do not have to make sacrifices to benefit others, as the morality of altruism demands. It is no sacrifice to give up a lesser value for a greater value, as we do when we trade. We do not have to make ourselves worse off to be morally good, as the morality of self-sacrifice implies. Morally virtuous people, says Rand, are egoists who are mindful of the long-term consequences of their actions but neither live for the sake of others nor ask sacrifices of anyone else.

The sin of self-denial

Traditional moral codes, she continues, mean putting ourselves into the service of some 'higher' authority, such as God or 'society' or 'others.' But you cannot expect to sustain your life when you pursue some goal 'higher' than life itself. Your life is your ultimate value, and to surrender it for anything else is not just self-sacrifice, but self-denial, and ultimately self-destruction.

Moreover, since value is the product of our reason, to surrender value is to surrender reason – that is, to surrender our own knowledge, judgment, and mind. If we are told that our 'moral duty' requires us to abandon our reason, warns Rand, we should realize that something is amiss, since reason is our essential tool for survival, and we cannot endure without it.

The evil of altruism

Yet this is exactly what the prevailing morality of *altruism* demands of us. It urges us to live for the benefit of others, praises self-sacrifice, and rejects self-serving action as immoral. This is part of many of the world's religions and is widely accepted as the 'right' way to live.

In altruism, the standard of morality is not the value of the action itself, but the identity of the beneficiary. Serving others is good; serving yourself is bad. But on that criterion, complains Rand, there is nothing to differentiate between gangsters and businesspeople. Both are called evil because they are both self-interested. Yet gangsters exploit others through violent force while businesspeople enrich others through voluntary exchange. There is no moral equivalence at all.

And do not confuse altruism with kindness, goodwill, or respect for others, she continues. Its core demand of self-sacrifice means self-denial. It makes 'morality' everyone's enemy. You can only lose by being 'moral,' because this 'morality' urges you to act against your own interests. That makes all of us look on others not with goodwill but with resentment.

Indeed, Rand observes, the state of our culture shows that the prevailing morality of altruism does not promote compassion and respect. Altruism encourages people to prey on others, to live off others, and to exaggerate their own needs rather than pursue their own success. The wealth created by dynamic individuals – at no cost to anyone else – is despised as a mark of their wicked selfishness. The logic of altruism is not that wealth should be distributed, but that wealth is evil and should be destroyed.

Altruism, then, tries to rationalize actions that are in fact immoral and destructive. And its attempt to suppress self-preservation and make self-sacrifice an obligation can only be achieved through the additional evil of coercive force.

The ethics of emergencies

Yet it is no sacrifice to help others whom you love, Rand advises. A man whose wife has cancer, for example, will willingly pay for medical treatment and spend time caring for her, because she is an important value to him. That is entirely consistent with egoism.

But it would be wrong to sacrifice yourself, or expose yourself to great risk, for a stranger. That would be to value your own life, knowledge, reason, and mind lower than theirs. There is nothing wrong in maintaining a general goodwill toward strangers, and it is entirely moral to help them in emergencies. But our help must not leave us worse off or put us in great risk.

And the circumstance must be a genuine emergency. It must be something unanticipated and not of the person's own choosing. Otherwise, our help merely encourages people's fecklessness. Also, the problem must be limited in duration. We are under no moral obligation to provide anyone with continuing support, as state welfare systems do. That merely encourages dependency and requires continuing sacrifice from others.

The importance of principle

So for Rand, the beneficiary of a moral action is the person doing it, not someone else. We should act in our own rational self-interest and expect others to do the same. Only this is true to our human nature and likely to promote our survival as whole human beings.

Reason, she says, makes humans unique in terms of being able to think, and plan, for their whole lives – and even beyond. So to deliver the maximum benefit to ourselves, we must think and act for the long term, not just for the moment.

This we call *principle*. A lie might get us out of trouble, but our fundamental values are not served by lying whenever we please, warns Rand: that produces only a tangled web of deceit and destruction. Our actions must consistently serve our longer-term goals. That means they must respect principles.

Moral principles may not be easy to define. For example, an action might be wrong in some contexts but not in others. It is not 'dishonesty' to lie to robbers about where your valuables are hidden. Their violation of your rights means the concept of honesty no longer applies. But if we can organize our principles into a consistent and context-aware scheme – a *moral code* – we give ourselves a quick guide to our concepts of right and wrong that helps us act in our long-term interests.

Three basic values

Your standard of moral value, then, is your own life as a whole human being – that is, as a rational being, says Rand, reason being the essence of the 'human' concept. *Reason*, therefore, is a basic value.

And this in turn means having *purpose*: knowing your own mind and long-term values. It means identifying your values clearly and ranking them according to their relative importance. Purpose focuses us on what is important, sparing us from constant searching, uncertainty, conflict, and drift.

To maintain your own life, you also need *self-esteem*. You need to appreciate that you are competent to think and worthy of life and happiness. You need to be able to respect the judgment of your own mind regarding reality and truth, and be confident in asserting it.

Objectivist virtues

Everything else in Rand's Objectivist ethics stems from these basic values of reason, purpose, and self-esteem. These values imply a total commitment to reality, placing nothing above it. They imply that our values, goals, desires, and even emotions must be validated by clear thought. And they imply that we must accept responsibility for our own actions. There is no supernatural being or mystical force to blame for our mistakes or correct our errors.

Virtues, explains Rand, are the practical actions by which we achieve value. To achieve values, of course, our actions must be rational. Indeed, the biggest *vice* – an action that destroys value – is to willfully deny reality and reason.

Virtue is not always rewarded. We can make mistakes about what action is right. Others might thwart our efforts. Events might overwhelm us. But over the long term, consistent, rational action generally benefits us.

The basic virtues

Rand's basic values of reason, purpose, and self-esteem all have their counterpart in specific virtues – the ways we achieve them.

For example, she says, we achieve the value of reason through the virtue of *rationality* – being consistently rational and actively accepting reason as our only source of knowledge, our measure of value, and our guide to practical action. This virtue requires an act of free will: it means choosing to use your mind, and choosing to focus your mind on what is true, neither drifting away from it nor trying to evade it.

That in turn implies the virtue of *independence* – accepting the responsibility of forming your own judgments and living by them. It also implies another virtue, *integrity* – never sacrificing your convictions to the wishes or opinions of others. It implies *honesty* – never trying to fake reality. And it implies *justice* – giving what is deserved, never seeking the unearned or undeserved, and accepting the full consequences of your actions.

We achieve the value purpose, says Rand, through the virtue of *productiveness*. This starts by recognizing that we sustain ourselves through productive work – not just living off our environment, as animals do, but shaping it to our own needs and values. Productiveness means more than merely working at some mindless job: it means consciously pursuing the fullest productive employment of your mind within your ability. To underuse your mind, she warns, sentences you to decay. You need to choose to work to achieve your values, and losing your enthusiasm for productive work means betraying your values and your life.

Self-esteem, similarly, is achieved through the virtue of *pride* – the recognition that you are your own highest value and that this value, like others, must be earned. That means building *character*, acquiring a sense of *self-worth*, shaping yourself on a moral ideal and refusing to sacrifice yourself for the sake of others.

The reward of virtue

Virtue's reward is happiness. But again, we must not confuse long-term happiness with fleeting pleasure. That would be to mix up very different concepts.

Gaining a value gives us pleasure; losing one causes us pain. Such sensations are a useful indicator of our immediate interests, says Rand, but are not necessarily a reliable guide for the long term. Alcohol or drugs or sexual promiscuity may give us temporary pleasure, for example, but if overindulged over a long period, they bring us only harm.

Instead, we must think actively and objectively about what is truly in our long-term self-interest, and make rational choices on that solid basis. We need to keep checking that our concepts are consistent and based in fact, and make sure that our actions correspond to what those concepts teach us – in this case, what promotes or harms our long-term interest. We may not always get the answer right, but if we can learn to think in this way, and resolve to do so, we have a much better chance.

True *happiness*, according to Rand, is the state of *non-contradictory joy* – joy that does not clash with any of our values. Not the fleeting pleasure of a whim, but the joy of achieving real values that are consistent with reality and our nature. This joy is our *purpose* in trying to live a moral life, and is the *reward* of objective thinking and the moral action we base on it.

The evil of coercion

Egoists can achieve their values and attain happiness, without conflict, through peaceful cooperation. But what happens when people disagree?

Rand considers it fine to argue with those we disagree with, to try to persuade them, or to dissociate from them if we cannot agree. But it is evil to *force* them to comply with our views – to coerce them into accepting our conclusions against their own judgment. That stifles people's use of their reason and therefore their capacity to live. Rational minds, insists Rand, cannot work under compulsion – that is why the freest periods in history were also the most productive. Force replaces creators with brutes and brutes with worse brutes.

Force, she continues, is also an attack on value. Values are facts judged by a rational mind. If you cannot think, you cannot value. A value forced on someone is not a real value: force cannot be moral.

By force, Rand means the initiation of physical force. It might be violence borne of fury, or silent coercion, or calculated fraud; the rational mind must reject them all.

But *self-defense* – retaliation in the face of force – is entirely moral. Those who initiate force renounce rational argument. The only answer to force is retaliatory force.

But retaliation can get out of hand. Victims may respond with disproportionate force or even blame the wrong person for their injury. That merely compounds the harm. We need some dispassionate agency to assess crimes and invoke proportionate restraint where it is due. And *that* is the function of politics.

8 POLITICS AND ECONOMICS

The principles of good social organization, says Rand, are an outcome of our moral principles, which of course are based on our knowledge and the reality that shapes it. Sound philosophy is essential to sound politics and economics.

Rational political principles

Rand's politics are based on *rights*, the links between our personal and social actions, which subordinate social actions to the moral law.

Rights are moral principles that specify when individuals may act freely, without needing anyone's permission. Rights do not require other people to do anything, apart from respect them: we cannot morally infringe someone's rights.

To Rand, rights stem from our nature as human beings. Our survival as whole human beings makes them vital to us. Life is our highest value and our moral standard, so the *right to life* is our most basic right. Without it, we cannot exist.

But there are other rights too. To survive and flourish long-term as whole human beings requires us to be able to think, to have values, to judge things, to make choices and act consistently on them, and to maintain our motivation and perspective – without others stopping us. That, says Rand, implies another right, the *right to liberty* – the right to choose to think and to act on our own judgment.

It also implies *property rights* – the rights to acquire, keep, use and dispose of material things that we value. Again, this is part of our nature: we survive not just by living off our environment, but by changing it, using technology such as agriculture and manufacturing. To survive we must be free to develop that technology and use the material goods that we produce. Curbs on property rights are curbs on life.

What rights are not

Rights, asserts Rand, are not something given to us by 'society.' They protect us against society. We do not have to 'pay' for our rights by 'giving something back.' Nor do our rights entitle us to anything from others. There are no 'rights' to a job, for example, or a home, or an education, or medical treatment, or welfare payments, because those would require other people to provide or pay for them.

Only individuals have rights; groups do not. Individuals are sovereign, not cogs in some collectivist machine. No 'collective' has any rights over their mind, effort, or product. That would rob them of what they need to survive as whole human beings. (And it would be futile, since only free, independent, thinking minds can be productive – which is why collectivism always fails, says Rand.) But respecting the rights of others to live, think, and produce benefits us all, because it promotes a creative, progressing economy and society.

The role of the state

Rights can be violated by the initiation of force. The only answer to that, as already mentioned, is retaliatory force. But we cannot safely leave that to victims, who may blame the wrong person or respond with disproportionate violence. So instead, says Rand, we agree to renounce our personal use of force and give the monopoly on force to an independent agency that can protect our rights by dispensing *objective justice* – the dispassionate, measured use of force against violators. We call this agency *the state*.

The function of delivering objective justice requires the state to follow clear and objective principles. For example, there must be objective *rules of evidence* to establish the degree to which someone's rights have been violated, and by whom. There must be objective *laws* that prohibit specific acts (not broad, vague concepts such as obscenity, blasphemy, and restraint of trade, says Rand) and objective rules on appropriate punishments. Such rules allow violence to be deterred, without excessive or misdirected force.

Another part of the state's justice role is to enforce contracts. Human beings are not lone animals, nor social animals, but *contractual* animals, Rand asserts. We engage in long-range planning, making agreements with others to advance our goals through collaboration and trade. But for that to work, people must keep their promises – and be forced to, if necessary. We also need a way to resolve any disputes about what was in fact promised. So again, rather than have people fighting over honest disagreements, we let the courts decide.

Government must be limited

In Rand's view, protecting our rights is the sole justifiable role of government. No other state functions can be justified unless *everyone* freely consents, since any purpose that is forced on someone violates their rights. So the state may not intervene in the intellectual or moral life of citizens, telling them what to think or how to behave. It should have nothing to do with production or distribution, not even providing roads, parks, hospitals, or schools.

This is not *democracy*, in which the majority decides what we do. Government is not the ruler of its citizens but their agent. Rather, Rand's vision is a *republic* based on the consent of the individuals who compose it.

We give governments a monopoly on coercion in order to protect our rights, but the potential misuse of those powers makes governments an even larger threat to our rights than criminals. For our own safety, government must be limited. This is the purpose of constitutions: to put limits on how a government can use its monopoly of force.

Such a limited, focused government would also spare us the evil of taxation. Rand insists that taxation, a forced removal of our property, is theft – not just of our money, but of the product of our mind. In a free society, she maintains, the money to maintain the few legitimate functions of the state could be raised voluntarily.

Other political philosophies

As we have seen, there is no 'right' to a job, a home, or welfare. It is perfectly moral for individuals to help others when they lack such things, but we cannot force anyone to do so. So there can be no automatic guarantee of security.

The idea of state welfare, says Rand, comes from the collectivist notion that we are each merely part of a tribe that has priority over us. It also assumes that the government knows best how to deploy the tribe's resources and has a 'right' to take them. But there is no objective way to determine who 'deserves' the forced support of others. In 'democratic' societies, the decision is made by majority rule. That, however, inevitably violates the rights of the minority. Rand sees it as no different from mob rule, where the largest, most brutal gang prevails.

She also criticizes *anarchism* – the idea that we do not need government at all – saying that it exposes us to predation by criminals. We cannot think and produce if we must live in fear, carry arms, fortify our homes, and form gangs for our own protection. Having a state sends the signal that there is no point in initiating force, because force will be returned.

And remember that even rational and moral citizens still need objective laws and ways of settling honest disagreements – which means they need a government.

Rand sees *conservatives* as another enemy of freedom and reason, basing their political views on faith and tradition. To her, faith is not a rational foundation for politics, and tradition is no guide either: today's political tradition is socialism – which is not what conservatives say they want. Conservatives have neither principles nor integrity, concludes Rand. They proclaim our rights, but violate them with policies such as forced conscription. They defend capitalism using the language of altruism, so they inevitably end up apologizing for their own ideals.

But for Rand, perhaps the worst political offenders are those who call for a *mixed economy*, a mixture of freedom and controls. That, she says, is not the 'best of both worlds' but a blatant contradiction. Though 'moderate' socialists and conservatives both advocate it, that is because they each want control: socialists want to control economic life; conservatives want to control social life.

So there is no consistent theory underpinning the 'third way' idea, and there are no principles behind its laws, goals, and policies. Nor is it compatible with limited government, since there are no boundaries to contain it. It allows rights to be sacrificed to short-term values. Pragmatism, not reason, determines whether rights are respected or infringed.

With no principles to guide the mixed economy, bogus 'rights' such as welfare entitlements are created at the expense of minorities. Pressure groups arise to grab their share of this legalized robbery. Controls are introduced, but then more controls are needed to tackle their malign results. Nobody's interests are safe. This is not a 'third way,' warns Rand, but a road to dictatorship.

A rational and moral economy

Rand describes *economics* as the science that applies political principles to production. A rational economic system, like other parts of human activity, must be rooted in correct concepts about the nature of the world and ourselves. And to be moral, an economic system must also respect rights.

Capitalism is the only moral system

The only system that does both, claims Rand, is *laissez-faire capitalism* – capitalism without any government intervention. Only capitalism respects people's property rights, making it the only moral economic system. It is also the only moral social system, since it respects people's rights and values. But a capitalist society is one whose citizens may still value art, science, or literature above material goods: *they* decide their priorities, not some authority.

Under capitalism, people pay their own way by creating value that other people want and are willing to pay for. Nobody has to sacrifice their life, liberty, or property for others. It is a just system in which other people judge what value you create, and reward you accordingly. It does not penalize virtue or reward vice by taxing those who create value and subsidizing those who do not.

Again, human beings cannot just live off the environment; we have to create what we need to live. Capitalism gives us the incentive to do so. If we produce value, others will reward us for it. And since nobody is forced to be our customer, and there are no laws to protect mediocrity, we must be *effective* producers.

This makes capitalism very effective at producing material wealth. The historical evidence, says Rand, shows how capitalism is a progressive force: innovation flourishes and wealth grows when people are most free – as they were in the Renaissance, for example, or in the great free-trade era of the nineteenth century.

Separation of state and economics

To preserve capitalism and its benefits, says Rand, we must remove every temptation for the state to intervene. There must be a separation of economics and state, akin to America's constitutional separation of church and state.

Certainly, there must be a framework of law, to protect everyone against force and to ensure that contracts are respected. Beyond that, there should be no laws or regulations over economic life, no taxes or subsidies, no scope for those in authority to exploit others or favor particular groups. This means people have to deal with each other as traders, voluntarily exchanging value – as equals, not as masters and victims.

In this laissez-faire economy, markets promote efficiency and value. Market prices, explains Rand, reflect people's free, rational judgments of what different products are actually worth to them. Markets encourage providers to seek out the least wasteful and most efficient processes in order to offer the best possible value to customers. Markets reward those who plan ahead, who innovate, and who create the best and cheapest products that attract willing customers.

Markets are therefore a continuous process of education, teaching us where and how to find value and efficiency. People who learn these lessons, act rationally, and make sound judgments reap the rewards. People who reject them, act irrationally, and have poor judgment do not. But they are the only losers: where state and economy are separate, nobody else is forced to bail them out or support their mediocrity. Capitalism encourages rationality.

The myth of monopoly power

There is a popular idea that capitalism enables powerful businesses to exploit the public or even to create monopolies, leaving customers no alternative but to accept their high prices and poor quality.

This is a caricature of capitalism, Rand counters. Any business that did try to exploit the public would quickly go bust as others rushed to offer better and cheaper products. Nor are monopolies either common or permanent. Even the largest company can be challenged, since capital markets make the whole world's capital potentially available to competitors. Or customers may simply switch to alternative products that serve the same need. You can only dominate a free market by continuously providing the best value.

Indeed, the most common cause of monopoly is government – through subsidies or regulations that kill competition or through outright state provision. State-protected and state-run monopolies certainly *can* exploit their customers, who they leave no other options. Statists may say that state corporations are run 'democratically' in the 'public interest' – but that, scoffs Rand, means only the interest of the ruling gang.

Economic power is real, she concedes, but it is not unique. Some people have more intelligence or education, giving them an economic edge over others. But at least their superior knowledge is not *stolen* from others, as the economic power of a state monopoly is. And in any case, economic and political power are quite different. Economic power is gained by offering others a *reward* – something they want. Political power offers them only *punishment*. It is clear which is evil.

The meaning of money

Rand believes that money, too, is widely misunderstood. To her, money is a tool of exchange – a tool for those who want to *create* and *trade value*. People accept money in the knowledge that they can exchange it, at some future date, for value produced by others. Its very existence implies the virtues of productiveness, honesty, and reason.

The expression 'The love of money is the root of all evil' comes from a time, says Rand, when it was power and force that made people rich. Under capitalism, though, money is a reward for thought, creativity, innovation, production, and value creation. It allows you to obtain what your effort is worth to others. Money is *made*, not stolen from others. It comes from others' non-coerced demand for your creative achievement. It is an entirely moral instrument.

But money does not confer virtues on those who lack them. It serves only those who understand its use in facilitating productive exchange and furthering their goals. Those without value and purpose, who get money through criminality or state power, will be corrupted by it. And those who apologize for their wealth will merely attract looters who will use state power to relieve them of it.

The critics of capitalism

Yet there is no shortage of people apologizing for their wealth, and for capitalism itself. Altruism is so rife that capitalism's defenders feel they have to portray it as an altruistic system, even though the two are opposites: capitalism is based on rational self-interest, altruism on (irrational) self-sacrifice.

Entrepreneurs cannot win by pretending to be altruists. They have no defense when critics brand them as selfish. Though they should feel no guilt about a system that creates and spreads value through entirely voluntary agreement, they retreat in embarrassment.

The moral justification of capitalism is *not* that it serves the public, says Rand – though it undoubtedly does. Pro-capitalist groups undermine themselves with this line of argument. The real justification of capitalism is that it is the only system compatible with a scientific, objective morality. Capitalism is the only moral system in history. It is the altruists who are the exploiters.

The irrationality of the status quo

In any case, objects Rand, most of the supposed evils of business are actually caused by government. The prospect of subsidies corrupts companies, and the established firms lobby for competition-destroying regulations that make life harder for smaller market entrants. In addition, regulations invariably have other damaging but unexpected results and give politicians and officials arbitrary decision-making powers.

Socialists, of course, believe that resources should be managed for the 'common good.' But there is no rational basis on which to decide what the 'common good' might be. Such redistribution also moves resources from those who create and manage them well to those who do not. Even more serious, says Rand, is the socialists' failure to mention that the key resources are not material objects but individuals themselves. Socialism therefore means controlling other people – which inevitably requires the threat of force. That is an assault on mind, reason, and judgment: it denies people what they need to function as whole, rational human beings. No wonder it has not worked.

And in the expression 'From each according to his abilities, to each according to his needs,' there is no *limit* to 'need.' The idea turns people into beggars and liars, encouraging them to exaggerate their miseries in order to benefit from any redistribution and to conceal their strengths so as not to be exploited by it. This can only damage our prosperity and indeed our survival.

9   RAND ON PUBLIC ISSUES

In a large number of articles and speeches, which make up a large portion of her written output, Rand applied her moral and political thought to the public issues of her day. These include healthcare, education, welfare, the student revolutions of the 1960s, racism, environmentalism, feminism, civil rights, laws on homosexuality and drug use, foreign policy, the Vietnam War and the military draft, terrorism and 'political' crimes, economic issues such as minimum wages, tax, planning, energy and inflation, and much else. Her views on each were highly robust, and it is interesting to look at some of them to see how her philosophy shaped them.

The poverty of progressive schooling

Rand favored Montessori education, which emphasizes independence, freedom – within rational limits – and respect for a child's natural development. She blamed many of our cultural problems on the 'progressive' schools movement, in which children who want to learn are instead told to play. The idea is to boost their social skills, but all they learn is to be part of the pack. Sadly, the rest of the pack are equally untutored.

And equally unjust: the child quickly learns that only today matters, because you cannot predict what the pack will do tomorrow. There is no point in building anything, because others will smash it. The only morality is the whim of the pack. The only value, they learn, is the ability to manipulate the pack to their own ends.

Teaching, where it happens, is not about imparting knowledge. It focuses on fantasy play – which denies reality. Or class discussion – which places value on whatever the pack agrees on. Or tasks of memory rather than understanding (e.g. learning the shape of whole words, rather than phonetics) – which overload children's minds with concretes without their learning concepts.

College and student discontent

The duller ones conform. Many of the brighter ones, bored and frustrated, simply give up. The last hope that someone might make the world intelligible to them is college. But here, says Rand, they are taught instead that nothing is knowable, that words mean what we want them to mean, that 'facts' are merely opinions. Teaching, again, is not done through lectures that deliver knowledge but through class discussion that flatters students that their uninformed opinions are as good as any expert's. So still they lack objective concepts to guide them.

This, Rand continues, leads students to demand more 'relevant' classes. But, trapped in concretes and lacking good abstract concepts, they think this means classes that are relevant to *today*, not classes relevant to life in the past, present, and future.

So it is no surprise that the majority, confused and demoralized, are easily led by activists with a political agenda.

Old Left and New Left

But this, said Rand, was the political agenda of the New Left – a political movement that sprang up in the 1970s and 1980s, with roots in the social revolution of the late 1960s. It was, she thought, incompatible with the ideas of the traditional or Old Left – and equally incompatible with reason.

The Old Left, she explains, claimed to be advocates of reason and science – albeit mistakenly. They thought that collective organization and 'rational' planning would bring general benefits. Socialism, with its more efficient factories and machines, would surpass capitalism. The economic power of capitalists would give way to the will of the people, all over the world.

But by the end of World War II, this productivity and growth illusion was shattered. The West was plainly outpacing the Soviet Union, so much so that the Soviet Union had to build a wall to keep people in. So instead, Rand continues, the Old Left tried to convince people that material prosperity was unnecessary because their collectivism delivered 'higher' values. Few were persuaded.

The New Left, by contrast, did not want to take over production but to destroy it, insisted Rand. Instead of promising plenty, they scorned capitalism for producing plenty. They sought a 'return of the primitive,' arguing that economic growth damaged a fragile ecology, that laws stifled human nature, and that drugs and Eastern mysticism would expand our consciousness.

The New Left, she argued, were clearly unconcerned with human welfare, or they would have embraced human nature. They wanted to be rebels but were actually the establishment – simply reflecting the prevailing view of humanity as a tribe whose members exist for each other. The prosperity of only some thus was deemed unfair. They had only platitudes and slogans to back them up, but so feeble was (and is) Western philosophy that, intellectually, it has been powerless to resist.

Racism as collectivism

The crudest form of this collectivist tribalism, though the New Left would reject it, is racism. Racism, says Rand, judges people not on their mind and achievements but on their ancestry. It suggests that values and character are determined at birth, and dismisses the essential characteristic of human beings – their rational faculty.

Racism, she observes, rises and falls with collectivism. It was strong in Nazi Germany, for example, and in the early Soviet era. That is because racism needs state power to maintain it, while capitalism breaks racism down. Capitalism regards each person as sovereign; markets judge them only on their productive ability, not on other irrelevant characteristics. It was capitalism that broke down racism and serfdom. In the US, slavery survived longest in the non-capitalist states of the South.

The welfare state and the mixed economy, by contrast, worsen the problem. They produce conflict between groups, which jostle for state favors: sectarianism and racism replace impartiality, and racial groups demand that their 'ethnicity' be respected, preserved, and supported. But this judges them by ancestry, and freezes their culture instead of letting it develop. Such demands, says Rand, are hostile to reason, rights, and property.

Environmentalism

The New Left willingly embraced environmentalism – because, claims Rand, it is a proxy for anti-capitalism. It betrays a naked hatred of production, achievement, and reason. And human life too: before manufacturing, life expectancy was short. Humans must keep advancing in order to survive, but environmental regulation stifles innovation. Rand sees such restrictions on productive technology as an attack on the mind and on life itself.

Environmentalists, however, regard progress as an assault on Nature. But their calls to 'leave Nature alone' are not radical, she insists; rather, they are deeply conservative. They are a veneration of the status quo – a demand to conserve everything except humanity itself. In Nature, getting even the essentials for human life is difficult; under capitalism, even luxuries come easily. Wealth and technology, not politics, will solve pollution problems. The environmentalists' real motive, Rand suspects, is a hatred of talent, success, and human achievement.

Civil rights

Rand's thoroughgoing defense of life and liberty nevertheless brought her to some of the same conclusions on civil
rights as the New Left. She saw abortion as the moral right
of a mother, since nobody else has rights over the disposi-
tion of her body, and since a potential human being is not
the same as an actual one.

She opposed America's self-sacrifice in the Vietnam War,
arguing that America had no national interest in the war.
She also wrote and spoke against the military draft. This, she
felt, was the greatest abuse of the power of the state – which
is established to protect people's rights. The most basic right
is the right to life, but military conscription demands that
individuals put their lives at risk, for a cause that they may
not even support. The draft shows that government has
given up its role of protector. Instead it promotes statism
– the idea that your life belongs to the state to dispose. As
for the counter-argument that 'rights impose obligations,'
Rand reminds us that rights do not have to be 'paid for' and
impose no obligation on anyone – other than the obligation
on others, including governments, to respect them.

Crime and terrorism

Rand also believes it wrong to criminalize people for their
beliefs and lifestyles. Crime, she explains, is a violation
of others' rights by force or fraud. Lifestyle choices, such
as sexual practices or drug use, are not crimes, because
they involve no use of force. Nor do ideas. A legitimate

government cannot punish people for their thoughts and beliefs: free speech is a right.

The initiation of force remains a crime, even if motivated by some political idea, insists Rand. Terrorists should therefore be treated as criminals, not as 'dissenters' or 'political prisoners.' To her, they are actually worse than everyday criminals because they corrupt the concept of rights, demanding to be called 'idealists' whose beliefs 'justify' the crime.

But if so, what beliefs justify what crimes? Plainly, this whole idea draws the state and the courts into deciding what political ideas are acceptable or not – which is itself despotic.

Economic policy

Rand sees government intervention in the economy as a sure way to unleash unexpected and unwelcome consequences. Minimum wage laws, for example, do not help the poor – certainly not the jobless poor. Rather, they raise unemployment because they set wages above the value that employers gain for the employee's effort.

Taxing the rich, similarly, does not improve equality (not that Rand sees that as a value) but reduces investment and therefore slows the economic growth that would lift everyone on its tide. Indeed, redistributive taxation simply takes property from people whose success shows that they can manage it well and gives it to others whose lack of material success shows them to be bad managers of precious resources.

But it gets worse. Redistribution and the welfare 'right' to economic security are a form of slave labor. If we demanded that people should work several hours a week for the state, we would call it slavery, says Rand. But when we take the fruit of their labor as money, we call it taxation. Is there any real difference?

Vague regulations, she insists, are a particularly damaging sort of intervention. In anti-monopoly legislation, for example, what counts as 'dominance' in a market cannot be clearly defined. So decisions come down to the arbitrary judgment of regulators. That encourages crony capitalism in which lobbyists and vested interests try to influence decisions for their own benefit. Firms therefore cannot predict whether a merger or acquisition, or even their own natural growth, will be ruled illegal by regulators. Because they cannot plan ahead, they become over-cautious, and future investment, productivity, and value is lost.

Foreign policy

Unfettered capitalism, Rand insists, is the quickest way to prosperity for all social groups. Capitalism's domestic foundations are minimal government and minimal laws, designed only to safeguard people's rights to life, liberty, and property. Its foreign policy is free trade – international collaboration between individuals and businesses who voluntarily exchange value.

Capitalism is often vilified for profiting from war, but this is wrong, counters Rand. Wars destroy capital, confidence, and commerce. It is only governments, she reminds us, that have the power to start wars and only governments that can force citizens to fight in them. Businesspeople cannot.

Rand thinks that war can be justified – but only for self-defense. But it was well past time that we stood up for rational values and ended the prevailing myth that governments are all morally equivalent.

The number of despotic regimes in the United Nations showed how much this idea of moral equivalence had taken root. Its acceptance had delivered half the world into communism – a collective ideology that places no value on individual rights and is, by that definition, evil. Is it morally right to take up arms against such tyrannies? Certainly, thought Rand – provided it was no self-sacrifice but was done to counter a real threat to oneself.

10 THE NATURE AND IMPORTANCE OF ART

Aesthetics – the theory of art – is another important part of Rand's worldview. Where *ethics* looks at what is *good*, *aesthetics* looks at how artists focus on what is *important* and turn complex abstract ideas into concrete forms that we can contemplate directly. It is about the principles by which this can be done.

Contrary to popular opinion, we can evaluate art objectively. This may seem a radical conclusion, says Rand, because we are told that art is 'personal' and 'emotional' and therefore not subject to scientific analysis. But that is because people do not understand art's *function*. The emotions evoked by art, like all human emotions, exist for a reason: they are important to our survival. Aesthetics is as worthy of scientific study as physics or biology.

The process of artistic creation

Rand explains the artistic process. Artists – such as painters, sculptors, novelists, poets, playwrights, dancers, or musicians – want to communicate something important. In their art, they isolate and highlight these essential elements. They focus on what they think important, leaving out what they think insignificant or accidental. For example, in painting an elegant woman, a portrait artist would not replicate a cold sore that happened to be on her lip at the time; that is accidental and irrelevant to what the artist wants to communicate. (But then another artist might well include the sore precisely to point up the futility of human vanity.)

By this selective process, the artist makes a re-creation of reality – not a fake reality but a sharper rendition of what the artist thinks is important about it. And potentially, that is knowledge: it could give us a better understanding of our world or a useful ideal that we might aspire to.

The critical role of art

This, says Rand, makes art critical to our survival as whole human beings. We acquire knowledge by forming concepts. A work of art can integrate many deep and complex abstractions concerning our very existence. By portraying these in a concrete form, it helps us to keep our abstractions firmly rooted in reality. And art's concrete form enables us to experience these concepts directly, allowing us to see the full, immediate reality of profound concepts. Works of art give us the opportunity to reflect on and contemplate deep reality and deep values.

To Rand, then, the very purpose of art is to communicate, through a re-creation of reality, things that the artist deems important – a worldview, a sense of life, an idea, or a judgment of value.

This, she observes, is why the history of art is a barometer of the underlying values of the civilizations that produced it. Thus the sculpture and literature of Ancient Greece, from a time of science and reason, portrays human beings as heroic, strong, beautiful, and confident. But the art of the Middle Ages, when humans were regarded as evil sinners, portrays them as deformed monsters.

The aesthetic purpose of highlighting important concepts through a re-creation of reality applies to all art, says Rand – whether we like the artwork or not. A work of art can teach you something profound that changes your life for the better, even though you may not want to hang it on your wall.

But few art critics understand art's rational purpose. Instead they suggest that art is something mystical that can be understood only by a cultured elite. This only encourages the profusion of meaningless 'modern art' that 'experts' claim is important – though they have no rational basis for any such judgment.

Art and life

Art can evoke powerful emotions. Rand attributes this to what she calls our *sense of life* – our subconscious view of life and what things mean to us. As we go through life facing choices and forming judgments, we develop general feelings about reality and life. Like concepts, the sense of life is a set of abstractions, but one formed subconsciously, not consciously.

It is this that explains our deep feelings about art. For example, some people might loathe the cold sore in the portrait as an affront to our ideal of beauty, while others may praise it as a just rebuke to human pride. The sense of life is not exactly an emotion, more a 'sense' or 'feeling.' But it is equally automatic, intense and personal, because it is about our deepest value – life itself.

The structure of art

To achieve its aesthetic purpose, says Rand, a work of art must have three key features. First, it must have a *theme* – the artist's message to the audience. For example, the theme in the paintings of the Dutch master Johannes Vermeer is the wonder of light.

Second, a work of art must have a *subject* – what the work is about. It may be heroic, or depraved, irrational, or mediocre, as the artist chooses. Vermeer's subjects (to Rand's disappointment) are humble domestic scenes – though to him they are only a means through which he renders, brilliantly, his theme.

The *style* of the work reflects the artist's own conceptual framework. It is the concrete form of a huge amount of abstraction. In the case of Vermeer, again, the precision of his style projects the ideals of clarity, discipline, and purpose.

Valid forms of art

Art's purpose, says Rand, can be achieved in many ways. Painting, for example, uses two-dimensional color to recreate reality – communicating to us through vision. Literature re-creates reality using language. Sculpture uses three-dimensional objects, involving both sight and touch.

Music, using sound and hearing, is slightly different. Music is a two-stage process: it grips us on the subconscious sense of life level; but then we can contemplate the ideals that the composer is trying to communicate using our reason. The same is true of architecture.

In the performing arts, such as acting and dance, the performers themselves are the medium. In ballet, for example, the artist attempts to convey strength and grace; in tap-dance, to convey precision and clarity.

Invalid forms of art

Rand considers some other forms invalid as 'art' because they do not comply with art's fundamental purpose of conveying a sense of life. Photography, she asserts, is not art – it is a technical rather than a creative skill. The decorative 'arts' are not art but purely sensory, not conveying any conceptual ideals.

'Modern art,' however, she sees as actively hostile to reason – and therefore to existence. Art, she reminds us, is about communication. A piece of 'modern art' might excite the senses, but if it is so stylized as to be unintelligible, it conveys nothing and therefore is not art. Indeed, by elevating sensory impact over the communication of thought, it is an attack on reason itself.

The principles of literary art

As a novelist and playwright, Rand was particularly interested in the principles of fiction writing. A novel, she explains, requires an additional element as well as theme, subject, and style. It needs *characterization*.

The *theme* defines the purpose of the novel. It is what expresses the author's worldview. That may be very wide (the theme of Rand's own *Atlas Shrugged* is the role of the mind in human existence) or narrower (the theme of *Gone with the Wind* is how the Civil War changed life in America's South). The theme is presented in terms of action – the novelist's re-creation of reality is what happens to the characters and how they react to it.

The novel's equivalent of the subject is the *plot*. This presents the theme as an unfolding story of events and action. The plot must fit with the theme and bring it to life in a purposeful progression of connected events. It cannot be haphazard or empty: the characters must be pursuing goals, and their choices must reveal the writer's purpose.

Characterization is the qualities of the actors in the story. Their character and motivations are shown through action and dialogue. They must act in accordance with their characters. Characterization, plot, and theme must be consistent.

The *style* of a novel reflects the author's view of human knowledge and how it is gathered. Style is a very personal matter, revealing the kind of mental functioning with which an artist feels comfortable. The writer's style may be to present the story in a very factual and literal way, like the Mike Hammer novels of the American crime writer Mickey Spillane. It might project a blend of reason and passion, as in works such as *Les Misérables* by Victor Hugo. Or, as in the work of the American novelist Tom Wolfe, it might present the material in terms of the author's own reactions.

Romanticism in art and literature

Romantic authors such as Victor Hugo produce novels that fit Rand's idea of art much more than those of Thomas Wolfe, which Rand calls 'a chaos of floating abstractions, of emotions cut off from reality.' The Romantic Movement, she explains, re-creates reality on the foundation of volition. What gives Romantic art its vitality, why it affects us so deeply, and why it is more morally charged than other movements is precisely because it recognizes, and seeks to show, that we have free will and that our choices and value judgments make a profound difference to us and to those around us.

Romantic art therefore does not focus on the mundane, or give us a mere photograph of life. It does not dismiss our choices as illusory or our actions as powerless against unstoppable forces. It focuses on the fundamental, universal, and crucial problems and values in life and on how we can and do deal with them. It aims to project a moral ideal: to show how things could be and *ought* to be – the aesthetic equivalent of ethics.

Romanticism affects us deeply because the crucial values and choices that it evokes stir our sense of life. Witness the intensely emotive work of the Romantic artists of the nineteenth century, who brought color, imagination, excitement, and originality into art and literature. The very best of them, like Rand's favorite, Victor Hugo, skillfully used character and action to highlight the most difficult choices we face in terms of our lives, values, and morality.

Deficiencies in contemporary art

Modern literature, complains Rand, has lost sight of the purpose of art, and of the crucial importance of volition, values, and emotions. It suggests that we are overwhelmed by outside forces and can achieve nothing. Hence modern writers' deep hostility to coherent plots, happy endings, triumph, or beauty.

Popular literature is also flawed, she believes, because it focuses on commonplace values, teaching us nothing. Its flawed morality – altruism – means that it can never convincingly resolve a plot. Too much popular cinema, meanwhile, is full of commonplace characters doing absurdly extraordinary things, characterization and plot are so inconsistent that any aesthetic purpose is lost.

The public, Rand asserts, is keen for Romantic portrayals, like the James Bond books of the British author Ian Fleming – though *not* the later films, which parody the hero. Genuine Romanticism presents a moral ideal that helps us to assert our fundamental values and meet the challenges we face.

Children, too, need Romantic ideals to develop their values. But most of what they read and see tells them instead to be altruistic and self-sacrificing – that morality is painful. The bright ones, seeing the contradiction, come to value nothing at all. That, she concludes, is the sorry state to which contemporary art and literature have brought our culture.

11 RAND'S NOVELS

The goal of Rand's fiction

To Rand, misery, disease, and disaster might be worthy of study but are not proper subjects for art. She thinks art should point out something positive: how things might be and ought to be.

As human beings, we have to spend effort on securing our physical and mental survival. We must discover the qualities of character that are needed in order to sustain our psychological life. Art can help us in that, though its value is not so much what we learn but the fact that it makes us experience and reflect on important subjects. That is what makes art a value in itself.

Rand's own purpose in writing fiction was to project, and make us reflect on, the concept of an ideal human being: to give us a model for our own lives, and the courage to grasp it. Such ideas pervade her writings.

We the Living

Theme and subject. The *theme* of Rand's 1936 novel (and later play and movie) *We the Living* is the individual against the state and the supreme value of human life. Its *subject* – drawn from her own experience – is the brutality of life when rational values are destroyed by the Russian revolution.

Plot. The *plot* shows an independent-minded young woman (Kira) finding a soul mate (Leo). The lovers try to escape the crumbling ruins of life in Bolshevik-controlled Petrograd but fail. Resigned to never escaping, Kira meets and has a grudging respect for an idealistic young communist officer (Andrei), from whom she gets money that she uses to secure medical treatment for the now-ailing Leo. But when Leo returns from his convalescence, he has lost his idealism and integrity. Andrei, meanwhile, torn by the contradictions between his communist ideology and the misery that it actually creates, kills himself. Now alone and having lost everything she values, Kira attempts to escape again but perishes in the attempt.

Characterization. In terms of *characterization*, this is perhaps Rand's most successful novel. There is depth to the characters that evokes the difficulty of the profound personal and political choices that individuals face when rational values are twisted by a perverse ideology enforced by state power. Undoubtedly, the semi-autobiographical nature of the book helps Rand to draw these events and characters. Like her, Kira is a self-reliant, individualist young woman living in revolutionary Petrograd – though unlike Kira, Rand managed to escape.

Style. The *style* is that of a philosophical romance, a form common in Russia and Europe but not in America, which is one reason Rand struggled to find a US publisher.

The characters discuss, and their choices and actions point out, the contradictions in communism and the brutal force that is needed to sustain it.

That, too, was not well received in 1930s America. But the book sold well in Europe and in 1942 was adapted (without her consent) into a two-part Italian movie (*Noi Vivi* and *Addio, Kira*). These movies were so effective in their anti-statist message that the Italian government, led by the dictator Benito Mussolini, pulled them from distribution shortly after their release. They were re-released in English in the 1980s, after Rand's death.

Anthem

For the same cultural reasons that made *We the Living* problematic for US publishers, Rand's short novel *Anthem*, written in 1937, was first published in the UK. One potential US publisher complained that Rand 'did not understand socialism' – remarkable for an author who had lived through the Russian revolution and indicative of the rosy view of state planning among US intellectuals in the 1930s.

Theme and subject. The *theme* of the book, said Rand, is the meaning of the human ego. Its *subject* is the escape from a nightmare world where individuals have been submerged into the state – where 'I' has been replaced by 'We.' Indeed, Rand originally intended to call the book *Ego* but feared this might give away the plot.

Plot. Rand thought *Anthem* had a *story*, rather than a plot. It revolves less around action than around changes in the characters' perspectives. Like other children, 7–2521

– names have been replaced by numbers in this world – is raised in a collective home. He has the 'curse' of being curious about things and a quick learner. He dreams of being a Scholar but is assigned a job as a street sweeper, which he sees as a punishment for his presumption.

He falls for a girl that he calls the 'Golden One.' He finds metal tracks in a tunnel that dates from the 'Unmentionable Times' of the past. Unleashing his enquiring mind, he uses this hideaway to conduct scientific experiments and discovers electricity and artificial light. He decides to tell the Scholars. But they say his invention must be destroyed: it would disrupt the work of the Department of Candles. He escapes to the Uncharted Forest, where the Golden One seeks him out. They find a house from the Unmentionable Times. He reads books from the library and discovers the word 'I.' They give themselves names – and make plans for a future in which people could, like them, regain their individuality.

Characterization. The lead character, 7–2521, discovers his individuality with and through another, the Golden One. This characterization is a mirror image of Kira and the early Leo in *We the Living*. Rand's first attempt to characterize an ideal human being was a female character, but in *Anthem* it is the male character that leads the action. There are few others in *Anthem*, except the Scholars, who uphold centralism and the irrational status quo.

Style. The book is written in the form of a secret diary. This allows us access to the hero's thoughts as he wrestles with his inability to conform to the collectivist state, and struggles to understand the concept of individualism and the profound choices it implies.

Anthem has some similarities with a 1921 Russian novel, *We*, by Yevgeny Zamyatin, and the better-known *Brave New World* by Aldous Huxley. In Huxley's book, children are also raised collectively and assigned to jobs. The only individualist, an outsider called the 'Savage,' is exiled and eventually commits suicide. But Huxley's is a world of planned plenty. He is optimistic on technology but pessimistic on human prospects. Rand, by contrast, predicts collectivist poverty. But in her world, there is at least the prospect of human redemption.

The Fountainhead

Rand's breakthrough novel was *The Fountainhead*, published in 1943. It made her famous, confirmed her position as a leading individualist writer, ranked high on the bestseller lists, and (together with the 1949 film) gave her financial security.

Theme. The *theme*, according to Rand, is individualism versus collectivism – not in politics but in terms of the human spirit. Indeed, unlike *We the Living*, there is no mention of politics or economics in the book; it is all about one creative man standing against a system that promotes mediocrity.

Subject. The *subject* is the battle for integrity and honesty in human creation. The battleground is architecture, and the hero who leads the fight is a visionary young architect, and pioneer of rationalist modernism, Howard Roark.

Plot. The *plot* opens with Roark being expelled from architecture school for his unconventionality. His conformist fellow student Peter Keating, meanwhile, gets a plum job at a leading firm, flatters the boss, Guy Francon, and is made a partner.

Roark eventually sets up his own business, but his buildings are ahead of their time and he is reduced to cutting stone to pay his bills. He meets Francon's daughter, Dominique, who also despises the mediocrity around her. They share a deep intellectual and sexual relationship. Roark gradually starts winning clients, but this provokes the influential *Banner* journalist Ellsworth Toohey, a socialist who hates Roark's individualism. He engineers a lawsuit, which Roark loses.

Unable to be happy in a world that does not appreciate Roark, Dominique marries Keating, But Gail Wynand, owner of the rabble-rousing *Banner*, becomes smitten with her, pays Keating for a divorce, and marries her. Intending to commission a new home for them both, he discovers that every building he likes is designed by Roark. He becomes Roark's client and friend.

Keating, though, now needs a big project to save his failing career. He persuades Roark to collaborate on a major housing project, Cortlandt. Roark agrees, on the condition that it is built entirely to his radical design. When Roark later discovers that Cortlandt's integrity has been ruined by the addition of conventional features, he dynamites it. Toohey and the *Banner* stoke public outrage.

At his trial, Roark persuasively tells the court how creativity depends on self-esteem and independence. He is sensationally acquitted. Wynand realizes that pandering to the mob was a mistake: Roark has succeeded despite them. And

Dominique, seeing that mediocrity *can* be overcome, leaves Wynand for Roark. But Wynand still asks him to design a massive skyscraper. The novel ends heroically, with Roark and Dominique atop the construction.

Characterization. The *characterization* revolves around five main characters. The hero, Howard Roark, represents creative individualism over collectivism: he holds that pure art is the work of an individual mind, and cannot be created by boards and committees. Peter Keating is the opposite. He is what Rand calls a 'second-hander,' lacking independence and getting his beliefs and values from others. He succeeds only through opportunism and cronyism. He has some ability but pursues wealth. He marries Dominique for self-promotion, not for love; his career rises and falls with changing fashions. The heroine, Dominique Francon, scorns the mediocrity of her father's firm. Only Roark is her equal, but Toohey has discredited him. Disheartened, she embarks on a life of self-punishment and misery.

Gail Wynand rose from childhood poverty to control a major newspaper. Like Roark, he is intellectually strong, but his success comes from pandering to public opinion – which is what eventually brings him down, losing everything, including Dominique. Ellsworth Toohey is Rand's personification of evil. He promotes collectivism and socialism with determination. Hating greatness in others, he tries to destroy the self-esteem of individualists like Roark. He says he supports the masses, but his real aim is power over others.

Style. *The Fountainhead* is a philosophical romance, written in a direct style that supports its rationalist message. The characters represent different worldviews and at points make philosophical speeches that explain them.

There was much criticism from American reviewers, unused to this approach. They saw the characters as unbelievable, one-dimensional mouthpieces, complaining that no real person would voice his evil motives as plainly as Toohey does nor boast the benefits of compromise as self-assuredly as Keating does. On the other hand, reviewers appreciated the heroic individualism of Howard Roark, which was rare in contemporary literature, and still is.

Many people come to *The Fountainhead* having read *Atlas Shrugged* and see it through the prism of the later book. This is unfortunate; though its subject is more limited, the key moral content is all there. It effectively evokes Rand's core values and virtues – reason, purpose, self-esteem, independence, integrity, honesty, justice, productiveness, and pride.

Atlas Shrugged

The 1957 *Atlas Shrugged* is the book that draws most people in to Rand's ideas. It was sensationally at odds with the collectivist mood of the times. But having already built up a large following from *The Fountainhead*, she found no problem getting it published, and it rose high up the best-seller lists. It remains hugely influential.

Theme. The *theme* of the novel is the role of the mind as humanity's only tool for survival. A sub-theme is the morality of rational self-interest – *ethical egoism*.

Subject. The book's *subject* is how most of the world lives by exploiting the few creative individuals on whom human survival depends and how life becomes impossible without those individuals' minds and reason.

Plot. *Atlas Shrugged* is a long book, and there are many complications and sub-plots, but the broad plot is very simple. Tired of being exploited and vilified, the world's most creative minds – engineers, inventors, scientists, academics – go on strike. Denied their creativity and knowledge, the world economy collapses.

The heroine, Dagny Taggart, is battling to keep and improve a family-owned railroad company. She is resisted by her brother James, who prefers to make cozy deals with incompetent cronies and to use political influence to thwart competitors. She teams up with Hank Rearden, another independent thinker, whose revolutionary new metal can save the railroad. They become lovers.

But their ambitions are hindered by the fact that key people they rely on are disappearing. These include the railroad's most gifted engineers and the major customer, Ellis Wyatt, who pioneered a way of extracting oil from shale rock but who simply sets fire to his wells and leaves. Another customer, Francisco d'Anconia, inexplicably bankrupts his own business, almost taking Dagny's railroad with it.

In the abandoned factory of the former Twentieth Century Motor Company, Dagny and Hank discover the remnants of a radically new kind of motor that could revolutionize transport and industry, but which had been destroyed. Dagny tries in vain to track down the inventor, but Rearden is facing the forced seizure of his metal by the government and regulations that forcibly break up his business.

Eventually Dagny tracks down the man she believes is behind the disappearance of so many key producers and follows him to his secret location. It turns out that he is John Galt – who is also the inventor of the motor. The secret hideaway is made invisible to the world by another of his inventions. Dagny falls in love with Galt but returns home, not yet prepared to abandon the world that Galt, Wyatt, d'Anconia, and the others have rejected. She discovers that, faced with worsening economic chaos, the government has plans to nationalize the railroads and seize steel mills and other industries.

The economic chaos continues, and the head of state prepares to address the nation. But his broadcast is interrupted by the voice of John Galt, who speaks to the nation instead. He explains that those who live by the mind are now on strike, justifying this with a lengthy presentation of Objectivist principles. He says they will not return until society recognizes their right to live their own lives and enjoy the fruits of their efforts.

When Galt is captured and about to be tortured by the looters' regime, Dagny finally joins the strikers. She and Galt escape and return to the hideaway. The regime eventually collapses, and those who live by the mind are at last able to return.

Characterization. Dagny Taggart is a gifted engineer and businesswoman whose ambition is to build and run an excellent railroad. Hank Rearden is a brilliant inventor and metallurgist who produces a revolutionary new metal. Ellis Wyatt, likewise, is an independent-minded oil prospector who is also an exceptional geologist and chemist. Francisco d'Anconia is a creative inventor, businessman, and thinker. (It is he who gives the novel its title, saying that in view of the state of the world, he would advise the mythical giant Atlas, who carries the globe on his shoulders, to shrug it off.) And John Galt is not just an engineer, but a scientist, inventor, and philosopher.

The plot and these characters illustrate Rand's point that human progress depends on inventions and breakthroughs, which in turn require knowledge, mind, and intellect.

These protagonists face a diverse array of antagonists. There is Rearden's wife Lillian, who constantly undermines him; crony capitalist Orren Boyle, Rearden's competitor; Floyd Ferris, a state scientist who asserts that science shows people have to be ruled by force; Dr. Robert Stadler, who allows his brilliant discoveries, and reputation, to be exploited by a tyrannical government; and Wesley Mouch, a treacherous lobbyist turned central planner. These characters illustrate the many ways in which mind and intellect can be sabotaged.

Style. Once again, this book is a philosophical romance, but it has elements of an epic saga. There is greater variety in the characters, particularly the antagonists. As in *The Fountainhead*, the heroine's love life is complicated but driven by the mind, not just the heart.

The antagonists in *Atlas Shrugged* are neither creative nor productive, so they live by robbing or leeching off those who are. But that requires the use of force, which is inconsistent with reason – humanity's essential tool for survival. And once they have ruined or lost the thinkers, they cannot endure. Rand is telling us that only by applying reason can we make the advances that we need to shape the world to our needs – be they the metals, engineering, or extractive and processing technologies of the story, or agriculture, medicine, and many others.

Creative minds discover new knowledge that improves our lives and promotes our survival. Their breakthroughs drive progress. Galt's strike shows that such minds cannot work under compulsion: they need to be free to create new ideas and new technologies. *Atlas Shrugged* shows that individuals' freedom to act independently is crucial to the whole of humanity.

The decline of the Twentieth Century Motor Company, related by a former employee as Dagny searches for the inventor of the revolutionary motor, is a powerful parable on Rand's views on the evils of altruism and egalitarianism. It was, we are told, a successful company until the founder's heirs gave it new principles: each employee would work according to his ability and would benefit according to his needs.

But the effect was that the harder people worked, the more they were expected to work to pay for their 'less able' colleagues' supper, or their child's measles, their wife's operation, their nephew's schooling ... with nothing to show for it. But who would decide what people's 'needs' actually are? A car? A yacht? And who would measure people's 'abilities'? It came down to votes at public meetings.

It was at these, the ex-employee recounts, that the workers realized that they had all become beggars. Nobody could claim rewards unless their 'needs' were greater than everyone else's. The meetings therefore became begging contests. Meanwhile, the company's output was falling: who then would work overtime to make up the shortfall? Of course, it was those judged to be 'more able.' The result was that everyone slowed down, determined to be less productive than everyone else, so they would not be called upon. Not only did it kill the company, it also destroyed the lives and self-esteem of those who worked in it.

And that, Rand is telling us, is the logic of collectivist ideology.

12 RAND'S CRITICS

Rand's philosophical approach

Modern philosophy, complains Rand, tells us that reality is either inaccessible, unknowable, or an illusion. So without anything firm to guide them, people drift into agnosticism, mysticism, and self-indulgence. Our rootless modern culture is ample demonstration of the fact.

But Rand's alternative leaves many critics unimpressed. They note that, except for *Introduction to Objectivist Epistemology* – a short treatise on concept formation – her ideas were laid out only in broad-brush articles and speeches that were not strong on details, counter-arguments, or evidence. Had she been a professional philosopher in a university, her ideas might have been tested in the furnace of academic debate. Instead, say critics, a coterie of admirers simply indulged and reinforced her views.

Critics also complain that Rand oversimplifies things. The fact that skeptics think that there are no objective truths to guide them does not mean all their actions must be a matter of arbitrary whim, as she suggests. They may act perfectly consistently, in principled ways, on the basis of their best *guesses* about how the world works. Likewise, the moral choices we face are rarely as stark as life or death. Most have little obvious connection to survival: they are things like whether to lie in order to avoid an unwelcome request or whether to return money that a stranger has dropped.

In addition, many readers recoil at Rand's hyperbole (e.g. 'The swamp is modern philosophy: the disinfectant is reason') and invective (particularly against Kant, whom she blames for almost every evil, including modern art). She is abrasive even against those who broadly agree with her on important issues (as Adam Smith did on capitalism, and even Kant did on free will).

Rand also presumes the worst motives in her opponents, say critics, branding them as weak, deluded, irrational, or immoral. She writes that altruistic societies are designed by and for 'parasites, moochers, looters, brutes, and thugs' – not language that is likely to win over doubters who believe their motives virtuous.

Rand on reality and knowledge

Rand builds her view of reality and knowledge on a commonsense foundation: that things exist, that they exist independently of us, and that we can know and understand them. Our brains tell us that things exist, but only by choosing to apply our reason can we know what they are. By creating concepts that group things by their similarities and differences, we can understand our world. But they must be good concepts, rooted in fact and reached by objective methods. We must guard against being subjective – which to Rand means *arbitrary*. A is A: a thing is what it is.

Though this theory of knowledge, which builds on a long tradition going back to Aristotle, should be taken seriously, many critics voice objections. Some, for example, point out that Rand's concepts are constructs of the human mind. But is the human mind a reliable tool for the job? It is itself, as a product of evolution, shaped by and part of the world. How can it soar above reality and give us an objective view of something that it is part of?

Other critics doubt that Rand's view sits securely on her three basic 'axioms' – that things exist, that we are aware of them, and that they have a specific nature or identity. Some regard these supposed axioms as mistaken: we could be living in a dream world where nothing exists. Others object that the axioms are so trite that almost anything can be built on them: most people would accept them while still reaching very different conclusions. Nor is it convincing, they say, for Rand to argue that you cannot challenge her axioms because you need to accept that things exist and have identity in order to construct an argument that they do not: again, we might be living in a self-consistent but illusory world. That may seem farfetched, but it at least demonstrates that a different interpretation of our experiences is theoretically possible.

Furthermore, the mantra *existence exists* does not defeat subjectivists, who rarely deny existence entirely. Rather, they assert that we have no *objective access* to the world, so our 'knowledge' of existence is flimsy. All we have is working theories – *guesses* – that, however well established, we must abandon when new evidence contradicts them. Rand of course accepts that we are fallible and might form concepts that prove mistaken. But then, if any concept can be upset by new ideas or evidence, how is her 'knowledge' any more solid than the skeptics' theories?

Moreover, Rand admits that as our concepts get further and further from raw perception, it is harder to be sure they are valid – though by assiduously tracing them back to perception, and checking them logically for consistency and non-contradiction, she believes they can be relied on. But critics argue that highly abstract concepts and relationships – such as the economy – simply involve too much information for any human mind to deal with. Reliable knowledge about such things is not just difficult, it is impossible. And our inevitable lack of knowledge is why attempts to redesign society or plan the economy invariably fail. There are limits to what we can achieve through reason.

Rand on morality

Rand's moral and political ideas are based on what she sees as the objective nature of things. We can reason out what actions are right from human nature itself. Morality rests on *facts*, not feelings: morality is objective.

Again, this idea that we can ground moral principles in the objective facts of human nature is profound, though critics doubt whether Rand really shows how we can move logically from *what is* to show *what ought to be* – the famous *is–ought* question that has eluded philosophers for centuries.

Her answer is that value exists for a purpose. It serves a profound need in us – the need for self-preservation. Having values is what keeps us alive. What serves our life is good; what thwarts it is bad. So forget feelings, opinion, tradition, or the diktat of authorities. The only standard for judging the moral value of an action is its impact on survival.

But *whose* survival? Rand talks of 'man's life,' but critics argue that 'man' could mean several things: our own species, humanity in general, the individuals who compose humankind, or any human individual. *Human survival* seems perfectly acceptable as a moral standard for how each of us should act. But Rand, say the critics, mistakenly confuses *human* survival with the survival of the *individual* who is taking the action – leading her to promote an egoism that most people would not accept as moral.

Critics also question whether Rand has properly understood the human nature on which she bases her individualist morality and politics. We are a social species, they say, and recent research on animal societies and genetics suggests that it is the survival of the *group* that matters, not of the individual. So it should be no surprise if we are programmed to act altruistically, and even sacrifice ourselves, for the general good – as many other animal species seem to do. And in fact, since we all share a genetic inheritance with other members of our species, what *looks* like altruism or self-sacrifice for an individual might actually promote the survival of the genes we have in common. Rand is therefore wrong to condemn apparently self-sacrificial actions, which – unseen by her – in fact promote the very essence of the individual.

But how do we know what promotes life, anyway? It may take a great deal of time and experience to work out what helps or harms our survival, and there may well be genuine disagreement about it. The Soviet Union, which Rand believed so harmful, lasted for decades and still has many defenders. Remember too, say the critics, that people in today's welfare states are living longer than ever before. By Rand's own standard of survival, the societies and life-styles that she scorns as parasitic seem to be doing quite well.

Rand on politics

Rand's political philosophy is as innovative as her ethics. The individual rights that limit the political process and guarantee our freedom, she says, rest on our knowledge of the world, human nature, and the principles of morality. They stem directly from what is good for survival.

But grounding rights in survival, say objectors, suggests that rights have no value in themselves and are justified only because they are useful. Yet as Rand herself argues, we have the right to act as we choose: she thinks, for example, that drug use and promiscuity are not useful – indeed, are damaging – but we still have a right to do them. So which is it?

Rand of course would argue that the right to experiment with different lifestyles – of whatever kind – itself has survival value. But many moralists would think it better to save people from self-harm (for example, by preventing them from smoking or eating fatty food or by forcing them to pay in to health insurance or pension plans). What evidence is there to justify either view as better promoting survival? How could we rationally decide who is right?

Stressing such limits to human reason, Rand's conservative critics say that she is too quick to dismiss religion and tradition as worthless. After all, they have brought us this far. That, say conservatives, is because religion and tradition each contain an acquired wisdom – knowledge of how we ought to act, tested and built up over the centuries and embodied in rules we do not have to think about nor even understand – but which nevertheless do promote the survival of ourselves and our species. We ignore these supposedly 'irrational' authorities at our peril.

Think of all those little acts of custom and politeness, of forbearance, generosity, and give-and-take, of seeing things from other people's point of view, of those minor self-sacrifices that promote mutual trust and cooperation and thereby benefit us all. It is hardly convincing to argue that all this can be squared with *egoism*, precisely because we know we will benefit from the trusting society it creates. We do it naturally, not because we have to think about it. That, not disembodied 'reason,' is our true nature. Perhaps, say Rand's critics, altruism has evolved with us, as part of our nature, because it does in fact promote our group welfare – though not in any way that we could rationally understand.

Rand on capitalism

Rand's defense of capitalism is again as innovative as her ethics and politics. Capitalism is, she says, a *social* system

– a form of society that does not just value material things, but values art, literature, and other non-material things too.

And capitalism is not something merely to be tolerated as a 'necessary evil' because it produces material wealth. On the contrary, she insists, it is the only *moral* social system, the only system not built on coercion. In capitalism, you acquire wealth by serving others, not by robbing them. Capitalist self-interest and profit are not evils; they are what motivate you to excel and to benefit others. Competition, too, drives the constant learning process on which human life depends – the process of learning how to create greater value at less cost.

Capitalism has its critics, but so does Rand's account of it. For a start, they say, capitalism grants us the freedom to trade in goods that damage us – such as tobacco. How compatible is that with Rand's ultimate standard of life?

And again, say critics, Rand seems confused about whether capitalism should be supported because it is itself a moral system or because it produces the best results. In judging political and economic systems, she gives considerable weight to outcomes – in particular, highlighting America's economic superiority over the Soviet Union. But it requires a long chain of evidence and argument to take us from rational moral values, through individual actions, then through social institutions, to such ultimate economic consequences. Individual freedom may be worth defending as a value, but can anyone really guarantee that it will produce a good and prosperous society?

Rand on art and literature

Rand's aesthetics are another innovation, and a potentially useful way of appraising art. Specifically, she says that true art gives important but abstract concepts a physical form that allows us to contemplate them directly. But her insistence on the rational purpose of art and literature is undermined, in critics' eyes, by her lavish praise of Romanticism, to the exclusion of all other possible movements – not to mention her praise for the American crime thrillers of Mickey Spillane, which few would classify as art.

Rand says that propaganda cannot be art, but critics point out that there is a no clear boundary between propaganda and the kind of moral education she believes that art can provide. Indeed, Soviet and Nazi imagery, sculpture, music, and architecture seem to be perfectly compatible with her guidelines.

Heroes may inspire, and Romanticism may have its place, say objectors, but an unbroken diet of either would quickly bore us. Art and literature that shows how *imperfect* human beings resolve their problems (and not always successfully) can be educational too – and probably more relevant and gripping.

Rand's fiction

Political cultures are rarely moved by novels, though Rand managed it. In line with her aesthetic principles, her novels are Romantic. They show individuals as heroic, or potentially so, and her view of what business, enterprise, and freedom can achieve is positive and inspiring.

Rand said that she devised her philosophy in order to write novels, though her novels certainly look more like vehicles for her philosophy. This, say critics, explains many of their faults as literature. Their plots are unlikely. The characters make over-long speeches to explain their views (John Galt's would last three hours, while Howard Roark's courtroom speech became the longest speech in Hollywood cinema history). At other points, too, the characters seem no more than mouthpieces for caricature views, often absurdly wicked or heroic. Few, if any, are morally gray. Indeed, Rand said she could never write detective stories because people would work out the good and bad guys straight away.

In terms of style, reviewers have complained of the length of Rand's books and the repetition in her dialogue – which they also say is rather 'left-brain': Rand tells us what to make of things instead of showing them to us and letting us work it out. Her tone is unsubtle: the antagonists are looters, parasites, flatterers, or villains; the heroes strong, principled, and determined.

Rand's novels portray the world as driven by a small number of creative people surrounded by a mass of aimless mediocrities bolstered by state power. But is that a fair picture? Do enterprise and inventions actually work like this? Even supposedly 'breakthrough' products, say objectors, are usually the result of a process of piecemeal improvement, involving the work and ideas of many.

Rand's novels may, as the critics say, be bad, heavy-handed books that pander to impressionable, mainly young, people who are seeking 'the' answer to life's problems. Perhaps so, but they nevertheless remain remarkably popular – and highly influential.

Ayn Rand's legacy

Rand's intellectual contribution

Whatever critics say of Rand's story-telling, people who read her novels know they are getting more than just a story. They are also getting a radically different worldview, with new ideas on life, personal morality, politics, and economics – all, she insists, built on the firmest of bases, the foundation of reason.

There is no shortage of moral codes and political visions rooted in the supposed authority of religious beliefs, in tradition or democracy, in the general approval of the public, or in the word of those in power. But all these boil down to matters of opinion: there is no objective reason to prefer one over any other. Rand, by contrast, insists, rightly or wrongly, that her own conclusions are rooted in the hard facts of reality: we can have moral knowledge, just as we have scientific knowledge, if we employ objective methods. And her choice to present these ideas through fiction makes them far more immediate and persuasive than any number of academic essays.

Rand also attracts readers for the robustness with which she defends her approach and the conclusions that follow from it – no matter how unpopular those conclusions might be. She tells us, for example, how altruism is immoral – that it makes success an evil and sloth a virtue, that it is destructive and anti-life. More than that, she actively asserts the contrary: that egoism or rational self-interest is morally right, that it minimizes the evil of coercion, and produces the best outcome for us all. And just to stir readers up even more, she calls this 'the virtue of selfishness.'

Equally robustly, she asserts that there are political and economic truths too, which can all be derived from the facts of reality and morality. She explains how a political system founded on individual rights is good in itself, reduces coercion, and (incidentally but happily) produces peace and plenty. Her argument for freedom is hugely innovative: that human beings are rational creatures, that our minds must interact with the world if we are to understand and improve it, and that liberty is therefore essential to human life. As is property: for us to prosper, we must be able to enjoy the rewards that come from using our mind.

Rand's fiction, above all, brings out the hero in her readers. If you have focus and self-esteem, she suggests, you can change the world. But self-esteem can be built only on real moral qualities and real character. She therefore urges self-reliance, grasping opportunities instead of demanding security, not trading your freedom or dignity to anyone, jealously defending your achievements and the fruits of your mental and physical effort, not asking favors nor being expected to make sacrifices, and respecting the right of others to live in the same way. It is a heroic vision that has moved many readers and changed many lives.

Against the consensus

Like all who court controversy, Rand attracts many followers but makes enemies of others. It is not only the content of her views that some find shocking, but also the way she expresses them. However many views there are on an issue, say critics, to her one is right and the rest are wrong. Compromise is unacceptable. Uncertainty is a 'revolt against reason,' while 'moral grayness' is a 'revolt against moral values' and the 'absolutism of reality.'

Such absolutism causes many to see Rand's views as more like a religion than a philosophy. Some of her followers have reinforced that impression, seeming to talk as if her methods reveal indisputable truths, with no possibility of error. But when religions, ideologies, authorities, and even sciences and philosophies claim to have certain truth, the result is often repression and tragedy, for who can reject what is true and good except those who are irrational or wicked?

Rand was a very resolute and charismatic personality. But criticism of her worldview does not mean personal criticism of her – and vice versa. Nor is criticism of a part of her system necessarily an attack on all of it, no matter how seamless it is supposed to be. Look beyond her charisma and the zeal it inspired in both supporters and critics, and there is much in Rand that is new, important, profound, and worthy of debate.

Is Atlas shrugging?

Rand's main influence, however, has been on politics and economics rather than philosophy. Her purpose for *Atlas Shrugged* was to prevent it from becoming prophetic. But the present state of the world seems almost beyond fiction. Some versions of all of the absurd and damaging regulations referred to in the novel are now in place in many countries. State ownership may be less fashionable, but state *ownership* is unnecessary when the state can *control* enterprises through subsidies, taxes, regulations, and threats.

The huge growth of intervention in the advanced economies does reinforce Rand's point that we have a problem of philosophy, not just of economics. We have come to accept that the only limit to state power is what the majority decide. That is because people and politicians do not understand the very specific and finite role of the state nor the coercive nature of majority rule and how that state coercion undermines the basic rights of all those in the minority.

Perhaps this lack of understanding is why so much of what is described in *Atlas Shrugged* has become reality. Capitalism and enterprise is being strangled by controls. The mixed economy has become a 'crony capitalism' in which firms and interest groups campaign for regulatory favors and subsidies taken by force from taxpayers. Though nominally free and privately owned, companies are shackled and directed by the state.

Rand's solutions are radical. She robustly rejects any use of coercive force and defends moral, political, and economic freedom. Her philosophy is not concocted to *justify* these policies; rather, her conclusions *follow* from her philosophy. She focuses on wealth creation because that, she believes, is the only way in which human beings, by their nature, can prosper.

Atlas Shrugged imagines a point at which the wealth creators and the other independent minds that carry the world on their shoulders would simply go on strike and leave the world to it. But there is little sign of Atlas shrugging yet. Perhaps the creative minds too have been absorbed into the prevailing moral and political culture. Perhaps they need philosophy themselves.

Understand the prevailing philosophical culture, and you can combat it and modify it, Rand tells us. Individuals really can change the course of history. Maybe not exactly as in *Atlas Shrugged* – which she acknowledged was fiction, not prophecy. But individuals can change events profoundly and enduringly.

13 QUOTATIONS BY AND ABOUT RAND

On herself

I seek to provide men – or those who care to think – with an integrated, consistent and rational view of life.

> *Playboy* interview with Ayn Rand

I am not brave enough to be a coward. I see the consequences too clearly.

> When praised for her courage in fighting the Establishment: quoted by Leonard Peikoff in *Objectivism: The Philosophy of Ayn Rand*

On reality and knowledge

[Objectivism] begins with the axiom that existence exists, which means that an objective reality exists independent of any perceiver or of the perceiver's emotions, feelings, wishes, hopes or fears. Objectivism holds that reason is man's only means of perceiving reality and his only guide to action. By reason, I mean the faculty which identifies and integrates the material provided by man's senses.

> *Playboy* interview with Ayn Rand

On the use of reason

Do you know that my personal crusade in life (in the philosophical sense) is not merely to fight collectivism, nor to fight altruism? These are only consequences, effects, not causes. I am out after the real cause, the real root of evil on earth – the irrational.

Letters of Ayn Rand, quoted in Jennifer Burns,
Goddess of the Market: Ayn Rand and the American Right

[W]hile animals survive by adjusting themselves to their background, man survives by adjusting his background to himself.

For the New Intellectual

Whenever you think you are facing a contradiction, check your premises. You will find that one of them is wrong.

Atlas Shrugged

There are two sides to every issue: one side is right and the other is wrong, but There are no evil thoughts except one: the refusal to think.

Atlas Shrugged

The middle is always evil.

Atlas Shrugged

On ethics

Every aspect of Western culture needs a new code of ethics – a rational ethics – as a precondition of rebirth.

'What is Romanticism?' in *The Romantic Manifesto*

All that which proceeds from man's independent ego is good. All that which proceeds from man's dependence upon men is evil.

The Fountainhead

On value

Learn to value yourself, which means: fight for your happiness.

For the New Intellectual

The man who does not value himself, cannot value anything or anyone.

The Virtue of Selfishness

On altruism

[W]here there's sacrifice, there's someone collecting the sacrificial offerings. Where there's service, there is someone being served. The man who speaks to you of sacrifice is speaking of slaves and masters, and intends to be the master.

The Fountainhead

The moral cannibalism of all hedonist and altruist doctrines lies in the premise that the happiness of one man necessitates the injury of another.

The Virtue of Selfishness

The purpose of morality is to teach you, not to suffer and die, but to enjoy yourself and live.

Atlas Shrugged

It is not self-sacrifice to die protecting that which you value: If the value is great enough, you do not care to exist without it.

Playboy interview with Ayn Rand

On self-interest/egoism

I swear, by my life and my love of it, that I will never live for the sake of another man, nor ask another man to live for mine.

Atlas Shrugged

An individualist is a man who says: I'll not run anyone's life – nor let anyone run mine. I will not rule nor be ruled. I will not be a master nor a slave. I will not sacrifice myself to anyone – nor sacrifice anyone to myself.

Textbook of Americanism

I shall choose friends among men, but neither slaves nor masters. And I shall choose only such as please me, and them I shall love and respect, but neither command nor obey. And we shall join our hands when we wish, or walk alone when we so desire.

Anthem

Selfishness does not mean only to do things for one's self. One may do things, affecting others, for his own pleasure and benefit. This is not immoral, but the highest of morality.

Journals of Ayn Rand

On virtues

A building has integrity just like a man. And just as seldom.

The Fountainhead

The man without a purpose is a man who drifts at the mercy of random feelings or unidentified urges and is capable of any evil, because he is totally out of control of his own life. In order to be in control of your life, you have to have a purpose – a productive purpose.

Playboy interview with Ayn Rand

The virtue of *Rationality* means the recognition and acceptance of reason as one's only source of knowledge, one's only judge of values and one's only guide to action... . It means one's acceptance of the responsibility of forming one's own judgments and of living by the work of one's own mind (which is the virtue of Independence). It means that one must never sacrifice one's convictions to the opinions or wishes of others (which is the virtue of Integrity) – that one must never attempt to fake reality in any manner (which is the virtue of Honesty) – that one must never seek or grant the unearned and undeserved, neither in matter nor in spirit (which is the virtue of Justice).

'The Objectivist Ethics' in *The Virtue of Selfishness*

On happiness

Hedonism is the doctrine which holds that the good is whatever gives you pleasure and, therefore, pleasure is the standard of morality. Objectivism holds that the good must be defined by a rational standard of value.

Playboy interview with Ayn Rand

Achievement of your happiness is the only moral purpose of your life, and that happiness, not pain or mindless self-indulgence, is the proof of your moral integrity, since it is the proof and the result of your loyalty to the achievement of your values.

For the New Intellectual

Happiness is that state of consciousness which proceeds from the achievement of one's values.

Atlas Shrugged

On emotion

What you feel tells you nothing about the facts; it merely tells you something about your estimate of the facts. Emotions are the result of your value judgments; they are caused by your basic premises, which you may hold consciously or subconsciously, which may be right or wrong.

Playboy interview with Ayn Rand

On politics and economics

On individual rights

Individual rights are the means of subordinating society to moral law.

The Virtue of Selfishness

Individual rights are not subject to a public vote; a majority has no right to vote away the rights of a minority; the political function of rights is precisely to protect minorities from oppression by majorities (and the smallest minority on earth is the individual).

The Virtue of Selfishness

Man's rights can be violated only by the use of physical force. It is only by means of physical force that one man can deprive another of his life, or enslave him, or rob him, or prevent him from pursuing his own goals, or compel him to act against his own rational judgment.

The Virtue of Selfishness

Any group or collective, large or small, is only a number of individuals. A group can have no rights other than the rights of its individual members.

The Virtue of Selfishness

A crime is the violation of the right(s) of other men by force (or fraud). It is only the initiation of physical force against others – i.e., the recourse to violence – that can be classified as a crime in a free society (as distinguished from a civil wrong). Ideas, in a free society, are not a crime – and neither can they serve as the justification of a crime.

The New Left

Never initiate the use of force against another man. Never let his use of force against you remain unanswered by force.

Journals of Ayn Rand

Observe, in politics, that the term extremism has become a synonym of evil, regardless of the content of the issue (the evil is not what you are extreme about, but that you are extreme – i.e., consistent).

The Virtue of Selfishness

Rights are not a matter of numbers – and there can be no such thing, in law or in morality, as actions forbidden to an individual, but permitted to a mob.

Capitalism: The Unknown Ideal

On property rights and creativity

Just as man can't exist without his body, so no rights can exist without the right to translate one's rights into reality, to think, to work and keep the results, which means: the right of property.

Atlas Shrugged

The basic need of the creator is independence. The reasoning mind cannot work under any form of compulsion. It cannot be curbed, sacrificed or subordinated to any consideration whatsoever. It demands total independence in function and in motive. To a creator, all relations with men are secondary.

The Fountainhead

The creator's concern is the conquest of nature. The parasite's concern is the conquest of men.

The Fountainhead

Let no man posture as an advocate of peace if he proposes or supports any social system that initiates the use of force against individual men, in any form.

For the New Intellectual

On the role of the state

Potentially, a government is the most dangerous threat to man's rights: it holds a legal monopoly on the use of physical force against legally disarmed victims.

The Virtue of Selfishness

There are only two means by which men can deal with one another: guns or logic. Force or persuasion. Those who know that they cannot win by means of logic, have always resorted to guns.

Philosophy: Who Needs It

The only proper functions of a government are: the police, to protect you from criminals; the army, to protect you from foreign invaders; and the courts, to protect your property and contracts from breach or fraud by others, and to settle disputes by rational rules, according to objective law.

Atlas Shrugged

The United States of America is the greatest, the noblest and, in its original founding principles, the only moral country in the history of the world.

Philosophy: Who Needs It

We are fast approaching the stage of the ultimate inversion: the stage where the government is free to do anything it pleases, while the citizens may act only by permission; which is the stage of the darkest periods of human history, the stage of rule by brute force.

Capitalism: The Unknown Ideal

Not only the post office, but streets, roads, and above all, schools, should all be privately owned and privately run. I advocate the separation of state and economics. The government should be concerned only with those issues which involve the use of force. This means: the police, the armed services, and the law courts to settle disputes among men. Nothing else.

Playboy interview with Ayn Rand

On capitalism

A free mind and a free economy are corollaries. One can't exist without the other. The dollar sign, as the symbol of the currency of a free country, is the symbol of the free mind.

Playboy interview with Ayn Rand

Wealth is the product of man's capacity to think.

For the New Intellectual

From the smallest necessity to the highest religious abstraction, from the wheel to the skyscraper, everything we are and everything we have comes from one attribute of man – the function of his reasoning mind.

The Fountainhead

Capitalism was the only system in history where wealth was not acquired by looting, but by production, not by force, but by trade, the only system that stood for man's right to his own mind, to his work, to his life, to his happiness, to himself.

Capitalism: The Unknown Ideal

In a capitalist society, all human relationships are voluntary. Men are free to cooperate or not, to deal with one another or not, as their own individual judgments, convictions and interests dictate.

Capitalism: The Unknown Ideal

The economic value of a man's work is determined, on a free market, by a single principle: by the voluntary consent of those who are willing to trade him their work or products in return.

Capitalism: The Unknown Ideal

Economic power is exercised by means of a positive, by offering men a reward, an incentive, a payment, a value; political power is exercised by means of a negative, by the threat of punishment, injury, imprisonment, destruction. The businessman's tool is values; the bureaucrat's tool is fear.

Capitalism: The Unknown Ideal

What we have today is not a capitalist society, but a mixed economy – that is, a mixture of freedom and controls, which, by the presently dominant trend, is moving toward dictatorship. The action in *Atlas Shrugged* takes place at a time when society has reached the stage of dictatorship. When and if this happens, that will be the time to go on strike, but not until then.

Playboy interview with Ayn Rand

On money

If you ask me to name the proudest distinction of Americans, I would choose... the fact that they were the people who created the phrase *to make money*. No other language or nation had ever used these words before... Americans were the first to understand that wealth has to be created.

Atlas Shrugged

So you think that money is the root of all evil? Have you ever asked what is the root of money? Money is a tool of exchange, which can't exist unless there are goods produced and men able to produce them. Money is the material shape of the principle that men who wish to deal with one another must deal by trade and give value for value. Money is not the tool of the moochers, who claim your product by tears or of the looters, who take it from you by force. Money is made possible only by the men who produce. Is this what you consider evil?

Atlas Shrugged

Let me give you a tip on a clue to men's characters: the man who damns money has obtained it dishonorably; the man who respects it has earned it. Run for your life from any man who tells you that money is evil. That sentence is the leper's bell of an approaching looter. So long as men live together on earth and need means to deal with one another – their only substitute, if they abandon money, is the muzzle of a gun.

Atlas Shrugged

Gold was an objective value, an equivalent of wealth produced. Paper is a mortgage on wealth that does not exist, backed by a gun aimed at those who are expected to produce it.

Atlas Shrugged

On prosperity

America's abundance was created not by public sacrifices to the common good, but by the productive genius of free men who pursued their own personal interests and the making of their own private fortunes. They did not starve the people to pay for America's industrialization. They gave the people better jobs, higher wages, and cheaper goods with every new machine they invented, with every scientific discovery or technological advance – and thus the whole country was moving forward and profiting, not suffering, every step of the way.

Capitalism: The Unknown Ideal

No politico-economic system in history has ever proved its value so eloquently or has benefited mankind so greatly as capitalism.

Capitalism: The Unknown Ideal

When I say capitalism, I mean a full, pure, uncontrolled, unregulated laissez-faire capitalism – with a separation of state and economics, in the same way and for the same reasons as the separation of state and church.

The Virtue of Selfishness

Every government interference in the economy consists of giving an unearned benefit, extorted by force, to some men at the expense of others.

Capitalism: The Unknown Ideal

On aesthetics

The skyline of New York is a monument of a splendor that no pyramids or palaces will ever equal or approach.

The Virtue of Selfishness

Art is a projection of the artist's fundamental view of man and of existence. Since most artists do not develop an independent philosophy of their own, they absorb, consciously or subconsciously, the dominant philosophical influences of their time. Most of today's literature is a faithful reflection of today's philosophy – and look at it!

Playboy interview with Ayn Rand

On heroism

Do not let your fire go out, spark by irreplaceable spark in the hopeless swamps of the not-quite, the not-yet, and the not-at-all. Do not let the hero in your soul perish in lonely frustration for the life you deserved and have never been able to reach. The world you desire can be won. It exists ... it is real ... it is possible ... it's yours.

Atlas Shrugged

I started my life with a single absolute: that the world was mine to shape in the image of my highest values and never to be given up to a lesser standard, no matter how long or hard the struggle.

Atlas Shrugged

The motive and purpose of my writing is the projection of an ideal man. The portrayal of a moral ideal, as my ultimate literary goal, as an end in itself – to which any didactic, intellectual or philosophical values contained in a novel are only the means... . My purpose, first cause and prime mover is the portrayal of Howard Roark or John Galt or Hank Rearden or Francisco d'Anconia as an end in himself – not as a means to any further end.

The Romantic Manifesto

Quotations about Rand

The fallacy in Objectivism is the belief that absolute knowledge and final Truths are attainable through reason, and therefore there can be absolute right and wrong knowledge, and absolute moral and immoral thought and action. For Objectivists, once a principle has been discovered through reason to be True, that is the end of the discussion. If you disagree with the principle, then your reasoning is flawed. If your reasoning is flawed it can be corrected, but if it is not, you remain flawed and do not belong in the group. Excommunication is the final step for such unreformed heretics.

Michael Shermer, 'The Unlikeliest Cult in History,' *Skeptic*

She was a wholly original thinker, sharply analytical, strong-willed, highly principled, and very insistent on rationality as the highest value.

Alan Greenspan, *The Age of Turbulence*

14 FURTHER READING

How to read Ayn Rand

Most people start with Rand's later novels, *The Fountainhead* or *Atlas Shrugged*. *The Fountainhead* does not deal with her political or economic principles at all, but is a good parable on her moral system. It provides a clear picture of her concept of an ideal human being – and of the virtues she upholds, such as integrity, honesty, and self-esteem.

Atlas Shrugged is longer and the explanation of her worldview is more explicit, being contained in (often long) speeches by the characters. According to Rand, the speech by John Galt 'is the philosophy of objectivism,' although its great length prompts some readers to skip it. And while the other speeches cover different parts of Rand's thinking, they do not unfold it in an easy systematic way.

It might therefore be better for a reader to start with at least some of Rand's articles and speeches, which are conveniently available in thematic collections such as *For the New Intellectual* (which includes a long statement of her philosophy and extracts from her novels) or *The Virtue of Selfishness* (focusing on the morality of egoism). For those who want to know more about the application of Rand's ideas, *Capitalism: The Unknown Ideal* (focusing on economic freedom) or *Philosophy: Who Needs It* (on rational thinking and its applications) would be useful places to start. All these collections are predominantly non-technical and easily readable.

However, Rand's articles and speeches were often written on the specific issues of the day, and for polemical effect. Within this large output, her points are often repeated or recycled in different forms. All this can make it difficult to see the coherent philosophical system behind them. But enthusiasts for Rand's novels argue that they draw readers into her philosophy. The novels, they say, provide an inspiring vision of how the world *ought to be* and (to use Rand's word) 'concretize' her philosophy by showing how her principles can be applied in practical situations.

Style. Some readers have difficulty with the fact that part of Rand's style is to shock. But philosophy and culture, she thinks, have become complacent and *should* be shocked out of it. So she uses searing language against those she disagrees with, including most of the leading figures in the history of philosophy. And she uses loaded terms (e.g. modern art is 'smears,' someone who fails to use reason is a 'savage'). There is usually very sharp thinking under all this, but some readers find the contempt and hyperbole distracting.

Another stylistic point that strikes the reader as odd is Rand's persistent use of 'man.' This seems sexist today, and it was even so when she was writing, as her use of it is so consistent as to seem willful. But there is a wider issue, because 'man' could mean an individual or something wider.

What is true of one may not be true of the other. It is easy to see the mistakes that can happen, along the lines of: 'Man domesticated animals 11,000 years ago, John is a man; therefore, John domesticated animals 11,000 years ago.'

Short guides to Rand

The following are useful short introductions.

Neera Badhwar, 'Objectivism' in *Arguments for Liberty* (2016, edited by Aaron Ross Powell and Grant Babcock)

Badhwar offers a short introduction to Rand's philosophy, and shows how it serves as an argument for a political system based in liberty of the individual.

Neera Badhwar and Roderick Long, 'Ayn Rand' in *The Stanford Encyclopaedia of Philosophy* (2010)

Brief academic outline of Rand's life, metaphysics, theory of knowledge, ethics, political philosophy, and aesthetics, including bibliography.

Andrew Bernstein, *Objectivism in One Lesson* (2008)

This short non-critical introduction assumes readers' familiarity with *Atlas Shrugged* and *The Fountainhead* and concentrates on Rand's philosophy, especially her moral system.

Harry Binswanger, *The Ayn Rand Lexicon* (1998)

A–Z explanations of individual terms and concepts in Rand's output. There is also a useful shorter version online.

Jeffrey Britting, *Ayn Rand* (2004)

> Short illustrated biography based on Rand's diaries and papers, focusing particularly on her influences and her resolute promotion of Objectivist ideas.

James Fitz, *Ayn Rand Universe: The Unofficial Guide to Her Life, Books and Philosophy* (2012)

> Short and neutral in tone, this is mainly an internet study guide, divided into very short sections. It is mostly biographical, with less material on her ideas.

Allan Gotthelf, *On Ayn Rand* (2000)

> Short, well-structured summary of Rand's philosophic thought, with extensive quotes from her essays and novels, including a brief biography.

Rand's main fiction

We the Living (1936)

> Semi-autobiographical novel set in post-revolutionary Russia, where values have been extinguished, with devastating effects on the lead characters.

Anthem (1938)

> Set in a dystopian dark-age future where individuality has been suppressed and technology is centrally planned, but the main characters find redemption.

The Fountainhead (1943)

> This story of an uncompromising architect who refuses to compromise his vision encapsulates Rand's view of the ideal man.

Atlas Shrugged (1957)

> Set in a dystopian US where creative entrepreneurs are hobbled by a culture of looting and leeching – until they decide to go on strike.

Rand's main non-fiction

For the New Intellectual (1961)

> The title essay sees the history of philosophy as largely promoting mysticism or force, rather than reason. There are also excerpts from her novels on subjects including invention and achievement, money, profit, and socialized medicine.

The Virtue of Selfishness (1964)

> Essays by Rand and Nathaniel Branden on the morality of egoism, the nature of egoism, the ethics of charity, and other subjects.

Capitalism: The Unknown Ideal (1966)

> Focusing on the morality of capitalism, this also has essays by Alan Greenspan and Nathaniel Branden. Subjects include the persecution of business, antitrust law, gold, property rights in the broadcast spectrum, the student rebellion, and the nature of rights and of government.

The Romantic Manifesto (1969)

Rand's exposition of the philosophy of art and her reasons for championing Romanticism.

The New Left: The Anti-Industrial Revolution (1971)

Robust critique of the 1960s and 1970s New Left movement, symbolized by dropping out, drugs, and revolution. Rand highlights its anti-success and anti-property foundations. There are articles on how progressive education binds and distorts the minds of children, on racism, and on nationalism.

Introduction to Objectivist Epistemology (1979)

Actually more limited in scope than the title suggests, this treatise goes into detail on Rand's theory of concept formation. Some technical language.

Posthumous collections

Philosophy: Who Needs It (1982)

These articles explain how important it is to have a philosophy, and that this philosophy should be conscious, rational and consistent. It illustrates this with essays on education, morality, politics and economics.

Return of the Primitive (1999)

Expanded version of *The New Left* with additional essays by Peter Schwartz on subjects such as feminism, multiculturalism, and environmentalism.

Rand in her own words

The Art of Fiction: A Guide for Writers and Readers (2000), edited by Tore Boeckmann

Concise advice for writers, assembled from talks by Rand, citing her favorites Victor Hugo and Mickey Spillane, as well as her own work.

The Art of Non-Fiction: A Guide for Writers and Readers (2001), edited by Robert Mayhew

Focusing on philosophically rooted factual articles, these lectures talk about developing style and the conscious and subconscious psychology of writing.

Ayn Rand Answers: The Best of Her Q&A (2005), edited by Robert Mayhew

Transcripts of audience discussions with Ayn Rand on a wide variety of topics, from modern art through racism, feminism, drugs, suicide, libertarians, and more.

Journals of Ayn Rand (1999), edited by David Harriman

These journals give insight into Rand's views on her life in Russia, her early career, and how she created her novels.

Letters of Ayn Rand (1997), edited by Michael Berliner

Generally chronological selection of Rand's correspondence, but with specific sections on her letters to Frank Lloyd Wright, Isabel Paterson, and John Hospers.

Objectively Speaking: Ayn Rand Interviewed (2009), edited by Marlene Podritske and Peter Schwartz

Transcripts of interviews from TV and radio shows, and with academics and journalists, focusing more on political issues than on her philosophy.

The Playboy Interview (1964)

Focusing on the practical implications of her worldview, this interview (with Alvin Toffler) provides a useful short insight into her thinking.

Books on Rand

Barbara Branden, *The Passion of Ayn Rand* (1998)

Perceptive portrait of Rand's personality and complexities by Nathaniel Branden's wife Barbara, who knew Rand for nearly 20 years.

Nathaniel Branden, *Judgment Day: My Years with Ayn Rand*

Unflattering portrait of Rand from her former lover and associate.

Jennifer Burns, *Goddess of the Market: Ayn Rand and the American Right* (2009)

Critical biography of Rand's life and role in US politics.

Douglas Den Uyl and Douglas Rasmussen (eds), *The Philosophic Thought of Ayn Rand* (1984)

Collection of academic essays from various philosophers, critiquing various parts of Rand's system, mostly from relatively sympathetic or neutral viewpoints.

Allan Gotthelf and James Lennox (eds), *Concepts and Their Role in Knowledge* (2013)

Academic essays, with comments and responses, on Rand's theories of perception and concept formation in science.

Allan Gotthelf and James Lennox (eds), *Metaethics, Egoism, and Virtue* (2010)

Exchanges between academic authors on Rand's metaphysics and ethics, exploring the connections between them.

Allan Gotthelf and Gregory Salmieri, *A Companion to Ayn Rand* (2015)

Comprehensive, scholarly reviews of Rand's output, including her novels, essays, speeches, and reflections on current affairs.

Anne Heller, *Ayn Rand and the World She Made* (2009)

Penetrating biography by journalist Anne Heller based on original research, new archive material, and interviews with Rand's associates.

Robert Mayhew, *Essays on Ayn Rand's Atlas Shrugged* (2009); *Essays on Ayn Rand's The Fountainhead* (2006); *Essays on Ayn Rand's We the Living* (2012); and *Essays on Ayn Rand's Anthem* (2005)

Scholarly, yet accessible, sympathetic essays on Rand's fiction, including its publication and reception.

Scott McConnell, *100 Voices: An Oral History of Ayn Rand* (2010)

Interviews with relatives, friends, and colleagues.

Leonard Peikoff, *Objectivism: The Philosophy of Ayn Rand* (1993)

Systematic and favorable outline of Rand's ideas, from reality and knowledge through ethics, politics, and economics. Written in philosophical language.

Tara Smith, *Viable Values: A Study of Life as the Root and Reward of Morality* (2000)

Rigorous, academic, but clear statement of the 'principled egoism' of Objectivist ethics and critique of alternative positions.

Tara Smith, *Ayn Rand's Normative Ethics: The Virtuous Egoist* (2006)

Detailed academic study of the fundamental virtues that Rand believes essential in order to achieve objective well-being.

INDEX

ABOUT THE IEA

The Institute is a research and educational charity (No. CC 235 351), limited by guarantee. Its mission is to improve understanding of the fundamental institutions of a free society by analysing and expounding the role of markets in solving economic and social problems.

The IEA achieves its mission by:

- a high-quality publishing programme
- conferences, seminars, lectures and other events
- outreach to school and college students
- brokering media introductions and appearances

The IEA, which was established in 1955 by the late Sir Antony Fisher, is an educational charity, not a political organisation. It is independent of any political party or group and does not carry on activities intended to affect support for any political party or candidate in any election or referendum, or at any other time. It is financed by sales of publications, conference fees and voluntary donations.

In addition to its main series of publications, the IEA also publishes (jointly with the University of Buckingham), *Economic Affairs*.

The IEA is aided in its work by a distinguished international Academic Advisory Council and an eminent panel of Honorary Fellows. Together with other academics, they review prospective IEA publications, their comments being passed on anonymously to authors. All IEA papers are therefore subject to the same rigorous independent refereeing process as used by leading academic journals.

IEA publications enjoy widespread classroom use and course adoptions in schools and universities. They are also sold throughout the world and often translated/reprinted.

Since 1974 the IEA has helped to create a worldwide network of 100 similar institutions in over 70 countries. They are all independent but share the IEA's mission.

Views expressed in the IEA's publications are those of the authors, not those of the Institute (which has no corporate view), its Managing Trustees, Academic Advisory Council members or senior staff.

Members of the Institute's Academic Advisory Council, Honorary Fellows, Trustees and Staff are listed on the following page.

The Institute gratefully acknowledges financial support for its publications programme and other work from a generous benefaction by the late Professor Ronald Coase.

In Focus: The Case for Privatising the BBC
Edited by Philip Booth
Hobart Paperback 182; ISBN 978-0-255-36725-7; £12.50

Islamic Foundations of a Free Society
Edited by Nouh El Harmouzi and Linda Whetstone
Hobart Paperback 183; ISBN 978-0-255-36728-8; £12.50

The Economics of International Development: Foreign Aid versus Freedom for the World's Poor
William Easterly
Readings in Political Economy 6; ISBN 978-0-255-36731-8; £7.50

Taxation, Government Spending and Economic Growth
Edited by Philip Booth
Hobart Paperback 184; ISBN 978-0-255-36734-9; £15.00

Universal Healthcare without the NHS: Towards a Patient-Centred Health System
Kristian Niemietz
Hobart Paperback 185; ISBN 978-0-255-36737-0; £10.00

Sea Change: How Markets and Property Rights Could Transform the Fishing Industry
Edited by Richard Wellings
Readings in Political Economy 7; ISBN 978-0-255-36740-0; £10.00

Working to Rule: The Damaging Economics of UK Employment Regulation
J. R. Shackleton
Hobart Paperback 186; ISBN 978-0-255-36743-1; £15.00

Education, War and Peace: The Surprising Success of Private Schools in War-Torn Countries
James Tooley and David Longfield
ISBN 978-0-255-36746-2; £10.00

Killjoys: A Critique of Paternalism
Christopher Snowdon
ISBN 978-0-255-36749-3; £12.50

Financial Stability without Central Banks
George Selgin, Kevin Dowd and Mathieu Bédard
ISBN 978-0-255-36752-3; £10.00

Against the Grain: Insights from an Economic Contrarian
Paul Ormerod
ISBN 978-0-255-36755-4; £15.00

Other IEA publications

Comprehensive information on other publications and the wider work of the IEA can be found at www.iea.org.uk. To order any publication please see below.

Personal customers

Orders from personal customers should be directed to the IEA:

Clare Rusbridge
IEA
2 Lord North Street
FREEPOST LON10168
London SW1P 3YZ
Tel: 020 7799 8907. Fax: 020 7799 2137
Email: sales@iea.org.uk

Trade customers

All orders from the book trade should be directed to the IEA's distributor:

NBN International (IEA Orders)
Orders Dept.
NBN International
10 Thornbury Road
Plymouth PL6 7PP
Tel: 01752 202301, Fax: 01752 202333
Email: orders@nbninternational.com

IEA subscriptions

The IEA also offers a subscription service to its publications. For a single annual payment (currently £42.00 in the UK), subscribers receive every monograph the IEA publishes. For more information please contact:

Clare Rusbridge
Subscriptions
IEA
2 Lord North Street
FREEPOST LON10168
London SW1P 3YZ
Tel: 020 7799 8907, Fax: 020 7799 2137
Email: crusbridge@iea.org.uk